# REINCARNATION
## The Evidence

**Also published by Piatkus**

*The Psychic Explorer*
by Jonathan Cainer and Carl Rider

*Your Psychic Power*
by Carl Rider

*The Power of Gems and Crystals*
by Soozi Holbeche

# REINCARNATION
## The Evidence

## Liz Hodgkinson

GUILD PUBLISHING

LONDON · NEW YORK · SYDNEY · TORONTO

This edition published
1989 by Guild Publishing
by arrangement with
Judy Piatkus Ltd

CN 4760

Printed in Great Britain

For Annie, with love

# Acknowledgements

For expert help and information in preparing this book, the author would particularly like to thank: The Wrekin Trust; psychiatrist Dr Denys Kelsey; Johan Quanger, editor of *The New Humanity Journal*; hypnotherapist Ray Keedey-Lilley and sister Jayanti of The Brahma Kumaris Spiritual University.

# CONTENTS

# INTRODUCTION

## *Delving into the past*

I decided to introduce myself to the subject of reincarnation by going to see two psychics, who claim to have the ability to see people's past lives. They both turned out to have very different approaches to their work.

My first session was with Soozi Holbeche, a healer who uses past life therapy to help her patients come to terms with difficulties in their present lives. Very often, she says, a deep-seated or chronic problem, such as a phobia, constant ill health, deep depression or lifelong difficulties with relationships can be resolved when a particular past life can be brought to the surface.

I asked Soozi about the healing she does, and she explained her work to me in these terms.

'When you understand why you act and react, you then have power over your life. My use of past life therapy helps the person who is being treated to bring together any unfinished business from previous lives that may be affecting them in the present.' Soozi said that a session with her would help the patient to take an objective overview of their life. 'If you're driving along a road in a car you only have a very limited perspective. However, if you follow the same route in a helicopter you can see the overall pattern of the surrounding countryside and can see your direction.' She felt that this illustration demonstrates how she sees her therapy – it enables you to step back from day to day preoccupations so that you can take stock of your life from a longer perspective. She emphasized that she is healing on mental, physical, spiritual and emotional levels.

When I went to see Soozi at her pretty flat opposite Kew Gardens it was a brilliant scorching hot day in May. Soozi is an attractive, well dressed woman in her late forties who became a healer after making a complete recovery from an accident which badly scarred her. She does not use hypnosis, but encourages patients to recall some significant past lives while still conscious.

As soon as I arrived she asked me to take my shoes off, go to the loo if I wanted to, and then lie down on the bed. She told me that the session would take about three and a half hours altogether. As I lay on the bed she put a large oblong crystal at each corner. She then put on some soothing music and explained her technique. She explained that for the first part of the session she would ask me some searching questions about my present life, and prod around various parts of my anatomy as she did so. If ever a particular prod hurt, or made me yell out in pain, I was to say, 'I forgive myself.'

'We unconsciously hold all kinds of traumas and repressed pains in the body', she explained. As I had told Soozi before the session that as far as I knew I had no illnesses or deep-seated phobias or fears, I was rather surprised that I did feel moments of quite excruciating pain at the various proddings. Soozi pressed hard on my right hand and I yelled out in momentary agony. She reminded me that I had to say, 'I forgive myself' out loud whenever I experienced hurt. The reason for saying this she said, was because the body stores or records the memory of all that has happened to it. When she is working, she is able to tune into any painful memories that the body has held on to. 'I forgive myself' means 'I release, or give away, anything negative that the personality has held on to.'

Soozi then asked me very detailed questions about my early childhood, my first conscious memories, my relationships, academic achievements, hopes and ambitions. Whenever I yelled out 'ow' she would say she could sense a trauma relating to age six, age eleven, age eighteen and so on, and then she would ask me to explain what this might be.

All this lasted for about an hour and a half. Every now and again Soozi passed one of the large white crystals on a thread about a foot or so above my body lying on the bed. As she did so, I sensed a definite coldness which almost made me shiver. It wasn't at all frightening, though.

One of the problems for me in undergoing this treatment was that I had to forget that I was a reporter, and actually be part of the session. Obviously I could not take notes, and Soozi discouraged the use of tape recorders. 'You're always worried about them clicking on and off and turning the tape over', she said. 'It means you can't concentrate properly on the session.' This was all very well, but I was worried about later recall. Not only that, but as we were doing it for 'real' I discovered that too many intimate details were coming out for public consumption anyway. What follows is the gist of what happened, and as much as I have been able to remember.

Soozi takes the phone off the hook when she is conducting a therapeutic session, as she says that it's very important not to be interrupted.

After a lengthy probe into my present life, we came to the past lives bit. I was by now feeling extremely relaxed physically, although still somewhat apprehensive. The very searching questions she asked had themselves caused a certain amount of mental pain, as I had to confront long-buried and at times rather uncomfortable memories. If relevant, Soozi asks her patients questions about their sex lives, how they received sex education, if they have had homosexual experiences. She also explores early childhood – parents, grandparents, sisters and brothers, and how these relationships helped to shape the present adult.

Soozi asked me if any past life came into my consciousness. I had to admit that there was nothing there at all. I was completely wide awake and also aware of a certain amount of backache from lying on the very soft bed and, possibly, from having to confront painful aspects of my past. As nothing at all swam into my mind, Soozi asked me to think of a number. Instantly, I said, 'nine'. She said, 'What do you see?'

I said, 'I see a small child, dark haired, wearing some kind of a tunic. The tunic is terracotta in colour, something like a Brownie outfit but it isn't a Brownie outfit.' I didn't instantly know the sex, although I said that the child had dark skin, not black or African, probably Greek. The child, who gradually seemed to be more female than male but who remained rather androgynous, was alone, although not unhappy. The time seemed to be very far back. Possibly it was ancient Greece but I couldn't be sure. I said to Soozi, 'I'm not sure whether I'm really seeing something or recalling something from a book I have read in the past.' She said that I was to carry on as it didn't really matter.

The child I was seeing was very serious and in some kind of temple or place of learning. Soozi then asked me to think of the number sixteen or seventeen and describe what I saw. I said, 'The child now appears to be female, although not very feminine. She has long dark slim limbs, and dark hair. She is very studious and serious and seems to be poring over books. They are like big leather tomes. Again she is alone but is not unhappy.' Soozi asked: 'Is she in training for something?' I said 'Yes, it seems like that, although there are no teachers around.'

The time then sped on a few years and the child had now grown up. She was surrounded by big leather books, studying and writing. The writing she was doing was not creative, though. Soozi asked, 'Is her writing philosophical?' I said 'Yes, I think so.' Soozie asked me to think of a number for when this particular life ended, and I said, 'twenty-five.' 'Was it a violent end, or was it illness?' she asked. I replied that there didn't seem to be any violence and I didn't even get an impression of illness, but that's what it probably was.

The next life that Soozi asked me to recall started with the number seventeen, but I can't remember anything else. As I was not allowed to use a tape recorder, that life came and went just like a dream that flashes by before you wake up.

Now Soozi asked me to think of my mother, not as she is now, in this life, but in a previous existence. Here, Soozi said, she may not be my mother, but could be my brother, sister, a friend, somebody in authority over me or somebody who is subservient to me. She asked me to imagine going down a long passage at the end of which was a door. What did I see when I opened the door?

I said that I could see two girls, aged about 13 or 14. They are dressed in Gainsborough-like clothes and I am the older one by a year or two. Soozi asked if the relationship was a comfortable one. I said yes, we were sisters, but then I qualified this by saying that I have been asked to take responsibility for this younger sister and I am finding this irksome. I like my sister but I find her rather silly in many ways, and I wish I didn't have to be with her all the time, and have to take charge of her.

Soozi then asked me to think of my relationship with my father in a past life. Again, he might not be my father, but could be in any relationship at all. She reminded me that he did not have to be male, even. Here I seemed to be adult and somebody in authority but not from a high class of society. I was a cook or a housekeeper, and saw myself in some kind of uniform. I was being plagued by this small boy who was a complete nuisance. He was an errand boy, or a butcher's boy or something, about eight or nine years of age and very mischievous. Asked how I felt about him, I said that I had no liking for him at all and regarded him only as a nuisance. Presumably, this was my father in another life.

Then Soozi asked me to think of another number. Instantly, I said 'twenty-five.' This time I appeared to be a young man, dressed in Jacobean style clothes, and brown breeches. I was good looking and intelligent although not a very nice person. I was clever and educated but did not come from a particularly elevated social class. I lived on my wits, by some kind of hack writing. I had a very sharp pen and a sharp brain but I was not very moral. I was not a criminal, but made a virtue of expediency. I was extremely sarcastic. Did I see anybody else with the young man who might relate to my present life, Soozi asked. 'Yes,' I said, I did. I saw a young woman who was clearly a close woman friend in my present life.

All these lives that I have just described were merely fragments. None of them was complete in any way. Soozi then asked me to go farther back in time. I said, 'I am now in the fourteenth century and I am a nun in charge of a convent. I am not old, in my thirties and although I am very efficient I do not seem to be a very warm kind of person. I am rather intolerant and unsympathetic towards younger nuns who are less perfect than me. I am rather stern and forbidding, not nasty, but somewhat unapproachable. More than a little scary.'

After this, Soozi asked me to describe the most miserable life I'd ever had. Here I appeared to be a very poor peasant, possibly in Anglo-Saxon times and was very unhappy and oppressed. I was in a kind of clearing and other people were around. I was very badly dressed, ragged even, and had a constant feeling of great oppression.

Soozi said, 'Can you see what life might have caused this very sad existence?' I said, 'I'm still in Anglo-Saxon times but now I am a very imperious lady treating servants and others quite badly. I am very untidy and make my servants work hard to clear up after me. At the same time I am very beautiful. I am also young. I am treating a particular young man quite badly.' Soozi asked if this young man was anybody in my present life. I said yes, this unfortunate young man – possibly a suitor – seemed to be my husband in my present life.

Next, Soozi asked me to describe the happiest life I had ever had, but I could see nothing here. She then asked me to imagine a shape of happiness, a bright light, enfolding warmth. But no life at all came to the surface at this point.

After this, Soozi asked me if I had any sense of misusing occult powers in the past. I said no, I wasn't getting any feelings of this nature. But she said that she was. She said that she could see me at some unspecified time in the past as some kind of sorceress. The nearest parallel she could find was the wicked Queen in Snow White, asking, 'Who is the fairest of them all?' In this life, I had been very manipulative and seductive, she said, and because of this, I had been very concerned in my present life not to misuse my powers. This had had the effect of making me put the brakes on myself at times and had given me a sense of 'handicapping' myself so that I would not be able to misuse the powers I possessed in any way.

When Soozi asked me which word swam into my consciousness when I decided to inhabit a female body in my present life, I said, 'handicap.' She explained this by telling me that because of my unconscious memory of being a sorceress in the past, I had decided to come into our present man's world as a female, where I would have a harder time than if I had been male.

She said that now I would be able to understand why I had on occasion handicapped myself – this has in fact been a pattern of my life and came out in the first part of the session – I would not need to do it any more, and the blocked energy could flow. We'll have to see if she's right!

Soozi finished the session by asking me to link hands in my imagination with my mother and father and then break the cord which still bound me to them psychically. Now we could all be free of each other. At the end of every session, Soozi said she brings together all unfinished business from the previous lives that have been explored, and heals and integrates them with the present life. She says that resolving the problems from your past lives that are affecting you in the present will make you master of your own life rather than a victim. Now, of course, I have no possible way of knowing whether I really was tapping into past lives, whether I was recalling fragments that I had read in books, whether the whole session was complete mumbo-jumbo, or whether profound truths were being imparted. There is no objective, scientific way of assessing this material. I would say, though, that whatever the reality of the 'past lives' might have been, many of the things Soozi told me about myself had the ring of truth. She was certainly accurate when she tapped into past traumas by prodding my arms, legs and hands. After the session I felt desperately tired and quite unable to work for the rest of the day. The session had lasted from half past eight in the morning until midday.

As I walked out of Soozi's flat and into the bright noonday sun I felt extremely disorientated. Soozi had asked me not to write down my account of what had happened for three or four days, so that the experience would have time to 'settle.' But when I tried to recall the session for this book, I found it all curiously like a dream. The fragments of past lives quickly faded away, and the only reason I know about them is that I did write down what had happened before the memories completely disappeared.

When embarking on a session like this, it is essential to be completely open and honest with the therapist. Soozi told me that many of her clients are nervous of meeting her again because they fear she knows too much about them, and has had access to all their innermost secrets. But she assured me that as soon as the session is finished, the door is closed and she forgets all about the confidences that have been revealed. She said she has to do this in order to avoid suffering from therapist's burn-out.

# Other lifetimes

According to my next session, I have been a Romanian gypsy, a communist rebel and an Indian princess in my past lives. These existences have been at the same time more exotic and far less comfortable than my present incarnation as an author and journalist. This information, plus considerable further detail, was given to me in a ninety-minute sitting conducted by Lee Ward, a Kent housewife and mother who has become very popular locally for her ability to see into people's past lives.

Lee reveals previous incarnations for her clients not as therapy – simply for interest and enlightenment. She does not use hypnosis, but looks into your eyes for a few minutes and then reels off, at incredible speed, a number of past lives. Her conviction is that we have all lived many, many times before, even if we don't remember anything about it. She has, she says, been granted the unusual privilege of being able to open the pages of the cosmic records, where details of all past lives are kept, and reveal the secrets that are contained within them.

Lee, in her early thirties, has been reading past lives professionally for six years. A lot of people who come to her are decidedly sceptical at first, she says, but many go away convinced that she is telling the truth. I too felt sceptical and more than a little nervous as I sat opposite her at the dining table of her suburban detached home in Canterbury. What would she reveal? Would it be at all frightening? What if I'd been a mass murderer in the past, or a thoroughly nasty character? 'Even if you had, it's all over and done with' Lee assured me. She looked at me for a few minutes, invited me to put on my tape recorder as 'I speak too fast for you to take notes or to remember everything', and then began.

The first lifetime she revealed to me was as a Romanian gypsy in the 1700s. Lee said that I was very unusual for a woman of that period, as during that lifetime I had never married. This was because of my brother. He had stolen a horse from a local lord, and had been forced to become a servant as a punishment for this crime, which was a great disgrace for a gypsy. I, his sister, had tried to rescue him and had been caught and seduced by the son of the lord. However, because of his social position he would not marry me, and I therefore remained single all my life. Subsequently, I became a leader of the gypsies, and was a much respected figure.

Having heard about this intriguing life, I was very keen to know what the life just before my present one had been like.

'Many of us,' Lee began, 'have had previous incarnations which only lasted a few years. If you die before the age of thirty, that's only a half life. I have to ask now whether there is an incarnation before the present one which counts.

'You can change sex in previous incarnations, of course, but in the life I'm seeing now you are female. I also feel very strongly that your colouring has remained much the same throughout your lives. You have always been dark, and I think you've been coloured at some stage – both Indian and African.

'In the particular life I'm seeing now you appear to be French and I think you are a communist as well. You are very Left Bank-looking, a strong character again. There is a masculine feeling about this character, although she's female. But you are not a leader in this life, you are more carrying out instructions.

'The time is in the 1930s, I think, and you are about twenty-one. You have been a communist since the age of seventeen and again, your brother got you into it.' This brother, Lee explained, is unlikely to have been the same one as in the Romanian gypsy incarnation. 'He could have been your mother in another life, or somebody unrelated. But that's another life, and I can't delve into it just now. But we do, for reasons best known to ourselves, keep coming into incarnations with the same group of people.

'In this incarnation, your brother is one of those who blows things up, dynamites things. We are talking about a Spanish area where all the problems were.' The Spanish Civil War? Lee didn't know, but said she got the feeling the time was somewhere between the two world wars. 'I don't know any history or geography', she went on. 'I just have to rely on what I can read in the pages of the cosmic records.

'You come from a farming background, not rich but not poor either. You are not well educated but have been taught to read, write and add up. An old man comes to see you, and you travel through the night to a mountainous region where your brother has been shot, although not fatally wounded. You tear a strip off your petticoat and help him with your knowledge of healing herbs.

'Once your brother is well enough you have to move on, spending the night at a series of safe houses, but not able to stay anywhere long as you are in an underground movement. They are after your brother, and you now decide to stay with him. There's this communist cell, and people are introducing you to other members of the cell. You are planning an attack which will make life better for the peasants. You are all revolutionaries.

'You do blow up a building – I can't say what it is – and you see terrible destruction all around you. You now have a gun, a kind of rifle, and there is the feeling that you are helping to release the peasants from servitude. You are giving them freedom, but their freedom may be that they have to become communists as well.

'You are watching all this going on and don't like what you see, but are told you are too young to understand. You and your brother and others become more and more like fugitives and are hiding in ditches. Every now and again you undertake little raids and you are thinking: this can't be right – we are living like criminals.

'I see you being chased and then reaching this village. You are going down a narrow street in search of one particular man, and the village is unusually quiet. You go down the street in twos and you are frightened. You can hear your heart beating. You see flares going off, and look up at a window to where the shutters have opened, and a gun is pointing straight at your brother. Then somebody comes out of the bushes and you are smacked on the head. You have been injured and fall unconscious. When you wake up you are in an underground cellar with a grating.

'You look out of the grating and see highly polished boots going past. There's a lorry, three or four lorries, and soldiers get out. We are in a Spanish area of France and the soldiers are in a Russian-type uniform. They are definitely not Spanish soldiers.

'It seems as if these soldiers have been brought from a port and then moved from there. They are invading the rights of the natives. You've never seen anything like these soldiers and can't work out what is going on. Then you see some of your own men, who have obviously been beaten, being put into the backs of these lorries.

'Then the bolts are drawn back from the door and this man is standing there. He is very well dressed and speaks in an educated although not native accent. This man is going to take you out of the cellar, but first you have to watch your own men being shot. This man feels that you will crack easily and takes you away for interrogation. He is sure you will tell them what they want to know. But you don't really know an awful lot because you are still young and have not been the leader.

'But because of the life you've been leading you are a war veteran, almost, and by this stage you are no more than twenty-five although you look forty. Your brother is now about to be shot and killed, but this man says they can save his life if you reveal information. Your brother signals to you not to, and is shot and dies.

'You are then taken away to a huge building in a nearby town. It's four storeys high with many windows. All the people in the building are wearing the same uniform that the soldiers in the lorries were wearing. You are taken into an interrogation room and bright lights are shone into your face. You are deprived of sleep but not actually tortured. When this man comes in, you spit at him.

'They already have most of the information they need, though, and the man is reeling off names you recognize. You become ill from pneumonia in this place. I can't say how long you are kept there, but you seem to be confined to this one room. Then the well-dressed officer comes in and says, "What a shame, you could have been attractive." You look at him and say that if ever you meet him again you will make him suffer. He tells you then you should have been a man as you are unbreakable in spirit, but that now your time has come.

'A doctor-type person comes in with this huge hypodermic syringe, the biggest needle I've ever seen. It's horrible. They plunge it into you and you can feel the fluid going into your arm. You can't stop them as your hands are tied, but the officer doesn't like the way you are looking at him. He looks away as you die. I don't know what the stuff is that they injected into you. But when people found your body, they thought you were about forty.'

This reading struck a chord with me, as I felt that it could explain my lifelong horror and fear of injections.

I asked Lee if there were any other lives between this one and my present incarnation, and she said there probably were: I might well have had time to live a short life as a child. 'At least,' she said, 'you haven't had a proper life since then. But at the same time I don't class it as a whole life because you died before you were thirty.'

After she had finished with this life, Lee looked at me again and then began on another incarnation. In this reading, she said that I had been the favourite daughter of an Indian prince in the twelfth century. I had rebelled against my family and had run away when my father had tried to force me into an arranged marriage with a man whom I detested. Eventually, I had ended up clandestinely marrying a healer and helping him with his healing work.

And there the session ended. There were some interesting links but I was surprised that Lee Ward had seen nothing which indicated any kind of writing career or interest in the arts, in painting and drawing or fashion, all of which have been with me since my earliest years. She said: 'These aspects probably were in some previous lives, just not in the ones which have come out today.'

I was also a little disappointed that I was such a completely obscure person in all these lives. I'd never been Queen Victoria, or Cleopatra, or a famous novelist, or fabulously wealthy, or remarkable in any way. Nor had I, apparently, been a man − which would at least have made a change.

Lee said: 'The overwhelming thing in all these lives is that you are very much a non-conformist. You don't like to be told how to do things, or what to do, and you very much do your own thing. You appear always to have been a rebel, and a strong character. Also, there is the wild, gypsy, independent streak running through all the lives.'

I came away mystified. Had Lee Ward really seen into my previous lives, or was she just very clever at assessing a person's character from their voice, manner and appearance as they sat opposite her at her dining table? Did she tell people what she thought they wanted to hear − or was she just operating as a channel, relaying information in much the same way as a radio or television set, which simply enables us to see and hear what is being transmitted? Certainly Lee sees herself as a channel − an impartial, objective medium through which information comes.

Obviously, I can have no absolute proof either way. I have never had any intimation of any previous lives myself, and the only thing that really connected past and present was the terror of injections. But lots of people hate injections − it doesn't prove I was injected with a fatal dose of something fifty or so years ago.

But the fact that Lee's revelations can never finally be proved or disproved makes them all the more fascinating. Although in the West we do not officially believe in reincarnation, many − if not most − of us do have a sneaking suspicion that we may have lived before, and may well do again, and that it seems highly unlikely that we live for eighty or ninety years at most and then snuff out for ever while life goes on for others.

Are there any real grounds for such a belief? Is there any convincing way of knowing whether I *was* once a Romanian gypsy who remained faithful to the memory of my aristocratic lover? To discover that, I had to look closely into the whole complex and ancient concept of reincarnation, a belief that has been shared − though the details differ − by many religions and cultures around the world.

# CHAPTER ONE

# *What is reincarnation?*

What exactly does reincarnation mean? Put simply, its adherents believe that all humans, and perhaps animals too, possess an eternal non-physical element which can never die, but which will enter a succession of suitable bodies time and again. The element which reincarnates is completely non-material – it has no dimensions and cannot be seen, touched or quantified in any way. Yet it is the most important part of us. It is the soul or spirit, the aspect which is responsible for our personalities and for the choices we make in life. It is this non-physical component, say reincarnationists, which decides where we will be born and how long we will inhabit any particular body.

Those who believe in rebirth compare the body to a suit of clothes or a car. When these items become too old to be of any use, or no longer give good service, we discard them and replace them with new models. But 'we' do not die along with the body. We simply wait a little while, and then find another new body – that of an unborn baby – to inhabit. The kind of life we have led in the previous existence will determine what kind of body we will inhabit next. According to some belief systems, human souls only ever inhabit human bodies, but according to other doctrines we might, if we have not lived a good life, reincarnate in the body of an animal or an insect or even a plant the next time round.

Does this all sound rational or logical – or so much nonsense? To many Westerners, the notion that we can incarnate again and again on the earth is a decidedly odd one. For many centuries the three major faiths which have dominated Western religious thought – Christianity, Judaism and, to a lesser extent, Islam – have categorically denied that such a thing as reincarnation exists. All these religions believe that humans possess an eternal soul, but teach that it only ever inhabits one body, after which it exists for eternity in the spirit world, in Heaven or in Hell – perhaps, according to Catholicism, after spending a time in purgatory first. But to most Eastern people, the idea of reincarnation not only seems logical – it is the only interpretation of human existence which begins to make any sense.

The belief in reincarnation is very ancient: in fact, it is probably the most ancient belief there is. All pagan and so-called primitive religions accepted as a fact that we would be born again and again into new bodies. They also accepted that it was the spirit, not the body, which was the most important part of any human. The body could wither and fade, but the soul or spirit was eternal.

Until very recently, most Westerners considered reincarnation a primitive, superstitious idea, something for which there was no shred of evidence or proof. Now, however, the concept is enjoying a tremendous revival: since the 1960s, the number of Westerners who feel they can no longer dismiss the idea has rocketed. Acceptance of this ancient idea has escalated at the same time as belief in orthodox Christianity has declined.

In the past decade or so, a number of film stars and celebrities have gone on record as saying they are now certain there is such a thing as reincarnation. The most famous of them is Shirley MacLaine, who has toured America with her highly popular reincarnation seminars. Other people who claim to have lived before have written extensively about their previous incarnations. Joan Grant, author of *Winged Pharaoh*, wrote seven books which she said were autobiographies of her previous lives; and the respected archaeologist Omm Sety claimed to have been the lover of an ancient Egyptian ruler.

Also, for the first time in history the question of reincarnation is now being investigated scientifically. Instead of dismissing the concept out of hand, scientists and psychologists in Britain and America are asking whether there is any possible way we can prove one way or the other whether reincarnation might happen.

Over the past thirty years, for instance, Professor Ian Stevenson of the University of California has collected literally thousands of cases from children who appear to have lived before, and who can clearly remember their previous lives. Professor Stevenson has followed up every single clue, identified the people concerned, and asked searching questions of everybody involved, in case the child or the parents could be making it all up for personal gain. His case histories are almost all of children, for the reason that it is usually easier to check out their stories: members of their 'previous' families are more likely still to be alive. Most of Professor Stevenson's cases are of children aged ten or younger, who would speak quite readily of their past life. In almost all instances, the previous person died an untimely or violent death, and the apparent reincarnation happened within months of the death.

At the same time as these world-wide investigations have been going on, other groups of people have been trying to establish whether or not humans do in fact possess a non-physical element, a soul. For although every single religion has accepted that the most important part of humanity is the non-material, non-dimensional aspect, nobody has yet proved beyond all possible doubt that humans do possess a soul or spirit. Religions and scriptures have asked us to take this on trust, but have not provided any evidence to satisfy the sceptical.

Over the past decade or so there has been serious research into aspects of parapsychology and into the near-death experience, where people who have undergone clinical death – in that their hearts have stopped beating – seem to float out of their bodies and enter a realm which is not a physical one. A large number of people who have undergone near-death experiences have come back to describe what it is like, although nobody as yet has ever come back from real death – so far as we know.

Those who object to the very idea of reincarnation ask why, if it exists, do so few people ever remember their previous lives? Also, they say, if we can't remember anything about our past life, what does it matter whether we have lived before or not? In any case, they say, there is no possible way of proving it one way or the other. To many Westerners, reincarnation investigation is in the same category as ghosts, apparitions, fairies at the bottom of the garden and astrological predictions – interesting, but at the end of the day, so much nonsense.

There is no doubt that reincarnation is an important belief. Once we take on board the possibility that we may have lived before, and might well live again, our attitude to all aspects of existence undergoes a fundamental change. All religions which accept reincarnation teach that as we sow, so shall we reap. In other words, there is no real way of escaping the consequences of what we have already done. After living one life, we come back into the kind of incarnation that we deserve. So, if we have lived a good life before, we come back into prosperity and health. If we have lived a bad or vicious life, we come back into appropriate adverse circumstances.

Whatever happens in this present life can be regarded as a direct consequence of what has gone before. This doctrine is known as *karma*, and is part and parcel of the idea of reincarnation. So for reincarnationists, there is no point in blaming our parents for the way they have treated us, or in blaming society for letting us be born into poverty. We have brought about whatever happens to us in this life by our actions in a previous existence.

Christianity and Islam both teach that if we are good, we go to Heaven. In addition, Islam teaches that those who die a martyr's death will go straight to Heaven. But how, we may ask, can justice in Heaven (or Hell) ever make up for injustice on earth? If an innocent person is murdered, or killed for a crime they did not commit, how can an eternity in Heaven make up for their life being cut short on earth? And does an eternity in Hell really make up for atrocious crimes a person may have committed on earth? How will justice ever be done to the six million Jews who died in concentration camps, for example? How will those who died heroes' deaths in wars ever be compensated adequately? And what about those thousands who are killed in accidents or earthquakes? How will Heaven ever make up for their life ending violently on earth? The non-reincarnationist religions have no logical answers to the questions of why there is so much injustice and unfairness in the world and why so many murderers seem to get away with their crimes.

But once we believe in the possibility of reincarnation, all these things can be seen in a different light. All reincarnationist religions teach that in some way we make for ourselves our circumstances on earth – if we are born into poverty, handicap or some other apparent unfairness, we have in some way brought these upon ourselves by what we did in a previous life.

But there still remain many questions about reincarnation. Even if we accept, in theory, that it might happen, who can tell us how? Does God, or somebody up there, keep a giant log-book of all our deeds and misdeeds, so that justice can eventually be done? Do we reincarnate instantly, or after many years? Does everybody reincarnate, or only a few people? Do we incarnate always into the same sex, or change around? Can we really incarnate into animal bodies? And what about those 'spirits' supposedly contacted by mediums such as Doris Stokes – haven't they reincarnated?

And supposing we do all reincarnate, how is it that there are so many more people around than there were, say five hundred years ago? Where do all these new souls come from? Is there a fixed bank of souls, or an endless amount? Is there any possible way of answering these questions so as to satisfy a scientifically trained, educated mind?

There is definitely a 'reincarnation craze' going on in the West at the moment. It all started in the 1950s with the story of Bridey Murphy, a nineteenth-century Irishwoman who had supposedly reincarnated into a modern American housewife. Then a number of hypnotherapists claimed to be able to regress people back into past lives, and their stories were told on television. The Bridey Murphy story and other claimed past lives have been extensively researched and analysed, and all this has intensified interest in the subject. Endless books have debunked the stories of claimed past lives; the one huge objection to these claims is, of course, that there is simply no objective way of assessing the evidence. You either have to believe that the story might be true, or dismiss it as rubbish.

But I believe that there are other, deeper reasons why we in the West are now interested in the possibility of reincarnation. There seem to be two main factors: first, that orthodox Christianity, which told people they must not believe in such a thing, no longer exerts quite such a stranglehold on people's beliefs, and second, that in the past three decades a number of Eastern religions have become immensely popular in the West. Transcendental meditation, Buddhism and movements like the Hare Krishnas, for instance, all base their belief systems on an acceptance of reincarnation. A large number of young people are now becoming interested in reincarnation, possibly because they can no longer accept what Christianity tells them.

Some people have said that the present Western interest in reincarnation is just a passing fad much like table-tapping, ouija boards or spoon-bending. Every now and again, they say, we become gripped by some rubbish like this – and then, just as quickly, the craze dies out. A century ago everybody was interested in spiritualism; then it was phrenology, the 'science' of divining character by the shape of people's heads; and after that it was Esperanto, the 'universal language'.

But I believe that the reason why we in the West have become interested in at least hearing about reincarnation is that, now more than ever, we feel the need to try to make sense of a world which seems increasingly senseless. Why are there so many wars? So many disasters? So many handicaps? So much unhappiness? So much sorrow? There is no doubt that a belief in reincarnation answers many questions about life which are otherwise difficult to answer.

A belief in reincarnation gives answers as to why we are born in such widely differing circumstances, why some children are born poverty-stricken and handicapped while others seem to have every privilege –

health, beauty, intelligence. It explains why some people are born far more gifted than others – for it is unarguable that some children exhibit miraculous gifts at very early ages. Mozart, of course, is perhaps the most famous example, but the papers are always full of stories of two-year-olds who understand computers without being taught, who can paint and draw brilliantly, who are terribly musical or precociously intelligent. Finally, a belief in reincarnation can answer the eternal questions: why am I here, where did I come from and where am I going? Those who do not believe in rebirth have no answers for these questions that everybody asks. But on the other hand, just because the doctrine of rebirth can answer these questions does not make it a fact.

A few years ago, like most Westerners brought up in the Christian tradition, I thought that reincarnation was complete and utter nonsense. In fact, when a friend whom I knew to be intelligent and hard-headed told me she felt certain it was the only thing that made any sense of human existence, I looked at her in utter incredulity. How could she possibly believe such a thing?

But now, having investigated the subject as thoroughly as possible given the current state of knowledge, I no longer believe it can be so readily dismissed. Of course, neither I nor anybody else has irrefutable, objective proof that reincarnation does or doesn't exist. But it has to be said that most Westerners who are contemptuous of the idea have never studied the subject or given it any serious thought. As soon as I started to study the idea of rebirth for myself, I found, like my friend, that it did make a lot of sense.

But before we can accept the idea of reincarnation, we have to believe that there exists a non-physical, eternal, spiritual element of humans which cannot die. It is not necessary to believe in God to accept reincarnation – indeed, for Buddhists there is no such thing as an all-powerful God – but we do have to acknowledge the existence of an eternal spirit, and to accept that this spirit ultimately has more meaning than the unarguably temporary body. Otherwise there is nothing to reincarnate. So we also have to ask whether the idea of an eternal soul in itself makes any kind of sense.

The point is that, ultimately, whether reincarnation happens or not, whether we have an eternal soul or not, is not a matter of belief. If we have eternal souls, we still possess them whether we believe in them or not. The same is true of reincarnation. If it is a fact, then we will reincarnate whether or not we believe in the process. The question is: can we know for certain either way?

At first the idea of reincarnation seems strange to most people because it is little talked about in ordinary society, and people who profess a belief in such an idea are often considered cranky or not quite right in the head. But once you take on board even the slight possibility that it might exist, all your previous ideas about human existence are changed for ever.

This book is not a personal quest, but an attempt to present the evidence both for and against reincarnation in as objective a light as possible. Reincarnation is assessed from the point of view of ancient and modern religions and belief systems; from the scientific evidence now available; from the stories of those who have claimed past lives; and from such techniques as hypnotic regression, by which deep-seated phobias and fears can be brought to the surface and dispersed by a knowledge that they really belong to a past life. The book takes a look at the largely American phenomenon of 'channeling', where people believe they are in touch with discarnate entities who dispense wisdom and eternal truth through their chosen medium, or channel. Such factors as ghosts, apparitions, the near-death and out-of-the-body experience and *déjà vu* are also discussed, as are current popular 'holistic' treatments such as past-life therapy and spiritual healing.

Above all, this book does not attempt to make converts to an essentially un-Western belief. But I believe it is now time to open our eyes to the fact that millions of people do sincerely believe in reincarnation, and ask whether that belief has any validity or not.

# CHAPTER TWO

## *Ancient beliefs and world religions*

Since the beginning of recorded time – about five thousand years ago – there has been a belief in the idea of reincarnation. It is, in fact, one of the oldest beliefs in the world and appears in ancient fertility rites and tribal religions in Africa, Australia, Ancient Britain and Ancient Europe. All ancient scriptures contain the idea of rebirth, and indeed for many centuries it was accepted all over the world as an absolute fact – something so obvious it did not even need to be proved. Most ancient religions and belief systems 'knew' that the body, which quickly and observably perished, could not be the most important aspect of human beings.

But although ancient beliefs shared the concept of rebirth, the hows and whys and wherefores were often very different. Some religions believed that humans reincarnated time and again so as to achieve eventual perfection. Others felt that this could not possibly be so, as people appeared to get more wicked, not better, as time went by. This idea is echoed in the story of Adam and Eve in the Bible: humans were once perfect, but then went successively downhill, spiritually speaking. Some Eastern religions asserted that every new fleshly incarnation meant a step further away from God.

Certain systems taught that reincarnation was species-specific – that humans reincarnated as humans and animals as animals. Most early religions believed that animals, as well as humans, possessed souls, and even those systems which did not accept that humans could incarnate as animals accepted that animals reincarnated in their own way, much like humans. Some religions, on the other hand, taught that we were reborn according to our deserts. If we had been specially good in one life, we might be reincarnated as a very elevated being, but if not we might have to endure a future life as a dung beetle or a worm.

Ancient religions all addressed the same questions: if we do reincarnate, exactly what is reborn – and how long after dying do we enter another body? Does the soul enter a new body at conception, at some time during growth in the womb – or after the baby is born? Do all souls reincarnate, or only the bad ones? In some belief systems, those souls which have attained perfection no longer need to experience rebirth and can go straight to Heaven. The Ancient Egyptians, for instance, held a number of beliefs about the afterlife and a return to a fleshly state was considered inevitable in some cases, even after a period of happiness on earth; they were the first to embody a systematic teaching about the immortality of the soul. The explanations were all very different and meant that for a long time rebirth was very much a matter of faith.

Most of the really ancient religions have been lost, and are of interest only to archaeologists and anthropologists. Their beliefs have not filtered down into any of the organized religions or systems that are widely followed today.

# Hinduism

The first great religion to codify a belief in reincarnation was Hinduism, which originated in the fourth millennium BC.

It is an extremely complicated belief system with very many aspects, and I shall concentrate here only on the basic belief in reincarnation as it is explained in the main Hindu scriptures, the *Upanishads* and the *Bhagavad-Gita*.

The *Bhagavad-Gita*, usually regarded as the Hindu 'Bible', is permeated with the idea of reincarnation and consists of a dialogue between the god Krishna and Arjuna, a prince waging war on the hundred wicked cousins who have usurped his kingdom. Arjuna is confused about the ethics of killing his relatives. The symbolic interpretation of this confusion is that whenever we have decided to live a higher, more spiritual kind of life, our old selfish, base tendencies or 'relatives' – the bad habits we have established over many lifetimes – are liable to intervene and try to stop us. They raise continual questions of doubt, fear and despondency. In Hinduism, it is a sin to feel sad or despondent – there is really no need for it, as all negativity is a reflection of our own ingrained bad habits.

According to Hinduism, each person possesses an individual soul which will go through a never-ending series of incarnations. Time is basically circular, rather than linear, which means that the world did not come into existence at some point in time but has always existed. Every few thousand years, therefore, everything will recur exactly as it has done before.

This means, in a sense, that everything is predetermined; an analogy can be made with music which is already in existence on a record, even though it cannot be heard unless the record is played. This belief, that everything recurs according to a set and unchangeable pattern, has led to an attitude of fatalism – that one cannot improve one's lot because everything is already determined.

When we die, according to Hinduism, what is left is a series of impressions on the soul, known as *sanskars*. These impressions are the result of all previous incarnations, including the most recent. Each incarnation leaves a deeper imprint, and will determine how the soul is next incarnated. It is the *sanskars* – the tendencies or habits – which are reborn and which are responsible for the kind of personality we will have in the next life. Hindu parents believe they are not responsible for forming the characters of their children – they are thought to be already well formed through their thousands of incarnations.

Hinduism takes the idea of *karma*, or cause and effect, very seriously. In simple terms, this doctrine teaches that whatever we do in one life will have an inevitable consequence. In the Christian ethic this has been expressed in the biblical admonition: 'As you sow, so shall you reap.' Hinduism explains the injustice and inequality in the world by saying that unfortunate individuals – those who have been born physically or mentally handicapped, or into poor circumstances – have earned this by their previous bad *karma*. They have accumulated debts which have to be paid off.

According to Hinduism, nothing perishes but continues to exist in one form or another: gods, people, animals, plants and minerals may all reincarnate. The concept of universal reincarnation is described particularly in Chapter 2 of the *Bhagavad Gita*. Everything, it says, is subject to the law of rebirth and nothing can escape it. Everybody is immortal, although very few people retain any kind of consciousness from one incarnation to another – only those with special powers can remember, or act upon, past life experiences.

In Hinduism, unlike Christianity, there is no intervening God or Jesus-figure to intercede for our sins. We are each responsible for ourselves and become how we believe: if we believe in ourselves as low, base souls, that is what we will become; if, on the other hand, we can see ourselves as elevated and divine, then we stand a reasonable chance of becoming better people. For Hindus, *karma* and reincarnation are more or less the same.

# Buddhism

The other great Eastern religion which accepts the idea of reincarnation as a fundamental tenet is Buddhism. There are many branches and offshoots of Buddhism, and all, like the various aspects of Christianity, believe something slightly different. Buddhism is different from Hinduism in that it does not include the idea of an immortal, ever-incarnating soul. Instead of a soul, according to Buddhists, people possess a collection of thought processes which can live on after earthly death and determine what life we will take next. General characteristics are maintained from one life to the next in much the same way as a river maintains its course.

In Buddhism, each new incarnation is a result of the past one but, it is not, as in Hinduism, inevitable. Nor should it be welcomed as desirable – indeed, just the opposite. Rebirth is a curse which humans bring upon themselves by behaving viciously in past lives. The more evil and 'earthbound' we have been, the more we have enjoyed and revelled in sensory experiences, the quicker will be our fleshly incarnation.

Each individual is said to consist of five separate sections: the physical body; feelings and sensations; perceptions, such as awareness and recognition; morals and ethics; and consciousness. At physical death all these sections fall away, leaving only a 'germ' of consciousness. This is what will be reincarnated, and the nature of the new individual depends on the quality of the aspects contained within this 'germ'. One's last thoughts as a sentient human being are very important for the next incarnation, as they will help to determine the nature of the rebirth. When conception occurs, it is not a question of a 'soul' entering the embryo, but of the foetus being moulded by the energy of thought processes from some previous life. The 'germ' is attracted to a specific embryo by some extremely complicated law of affinity, so that your next birth will be the one that is exactly right for you.

In Tibetan Buddhism it is believed that the two highest Lamas, the Dalai and Panchen Lamas, reincarnate according to set laws. Therefore as soon as one of these important figures dies, a search is initiated for his successor. Although most religions that accept reincarnation believe that the soul is without gender, the new incarnation of the Lama is always male. The present Dalai Lama was reincarnated two years after his predecessor died in 1933, and was pronounced the next Dalai Lama at the age of two, in 1937.

For Buddhists, the religious life is a necessity as it helps them to escape the constant cycle of birth and rebirth by overcoming all desires and negative emotions. The only reality in Buddhism is Nirvana, the state of not being reborn. The popular Western idea of Nirvana is that it is nothingness, but Buddhists see it as a state of ultimate truth, a condition in which the soul or 'germ' has passed beyond passion, desire and the craving for individual satisfaction. But for most people, Nirvana is too hard to attain.

# Jainism

Most Westerners know Jains as the peculiar people who walk along the street with brushes so that they can gently sweep away everything in their path, in case they accidentally tread on an animal or insect and kill it. In fact Jainism is a very ancient religion going back to 600 BC, and has much in common with Hinduism.

One of its central beliefs is that through successive incarnations the soul picks up many vicious habits and traits, much like a car collects dirt on a long journey. Originally the soul started out perfect, but its many fleshly habitations mean that it becomes overlaid with impurities; however, it remains pure underneath. Jainism shows people how to regain their original purity.

As with Hinduism and Buddhism, Jains believe that it is basically *Karma* that causes souls to reincarnate. As we accumulate debts, so these have to be paid off in future lives, inevitably and inexorably. The one sure way of atoning for the past is to live a life of religious austerity whereby all desires, passions and bondages to other people, as well as former vicious habits, can be overcome, and the soul enabled to return to its state of former purity. True liberation occurs when the soul is freed from having to worry itself about physical matters and all that that implies.

# Sikhism

*Sikhism*, which was founded in the fifteenth century by Nanak, also believes implicitly in reincarnation.

# Shintoism

In early Shintoism, which was the indigenous religion of Japan, there seems at first to have been no particular doctrine of reincarnation. The spirits of the dead continued to exist in much the same way as they had when enclosed in a physical body. The wicked would remain wicked and haunt the earth, while the good spirits would do good. After physical death, human spirits mingled with the rest of nature and became part of it. Early Shintoism emphasizes the 'oneness' of everything.

Then in the twelfth century Buddhism came to Japan, and brought with it the doctrines of *karma* and reincarnation. These became assimilated into traditional Shintoism, so that adherents came to believe that people are reincarnated after death, rather than melt back into nature.

Modern Shintoism has many forms and the imperial variety is forbidden to the general public.

# Ancient Greece

Moving now towards the West, the Ancient Greeks believed in the idea of transmigration of souls. This belief, which originated in the sixth century BC with the Orphics, held, like the Eastern religions, that this life on earth was illusion, that the true reality was the life beyond fleshly incarnation. The soul could only go to its true home after death, but in most cases it was quickly reimprisoned in another body, which could be either human or animal. The philosopher and mathematician Pythagoras, believed in past lives and was able to recall his own.

Plato also mentions rebirth in many of his books. His basic belief was that the soul is immortal and its true home is not when imprisoned within a body, but when free of matter in the upper air. According to Plato, there existed a fixed number of souls to incarnate, and the manner of successive incarnations depended on what kind of life had been lived previously. As with Buddhism, those who are attracted to earthly delights will reincarnate quickly after death and under worse conditions than before. In fact, the more sensually orientated and 'unspiritual' a person, the more coarse and animal-like will be the next incarnation. Those who are extremely wicked will certainly be reborn as an animal. But if the animal then lives a virtuous life, the soul may progress back up the scale until it is incarnated as a human once more. In Platonism reincarnation is not endless, as the soul does not always maintain enough energy to be incarnated again and again.

Aristotle began by accepting the concept of rebirth, but later rejected it. He taught instead that the normal state of the soul was existence without a body, and that to be captured in a human frame was a serious illness, an aberration.

## Judaism

On the whole neither Jews nor Muslims believe in reincarnation, although in both religions there are certain arcane traditions which take on board this possibility. The esoteric form of Judaism, the Kabbala, meaning 'traditional law', holds that souls are subject to transmigration, and that many souls and spirits may incarnate again and again without ever going to Heaven. It is only those souls which can attain perfection in this life which will escape reincarnation but souls that have not developed any kind of perfection must live life after life until they are worthy of being united with God for ever.

## Islam

Modern Islam does not embrace reincarnation, but states that all souls have only one earthly life before going to Heaven for ever. However, the Sufi sect, who represent the mystical side of Islam, have retained a belief in rebirth.

Sufis believe that their version of Islam is several centuries older than that supposedly revealed to the prophet Mohammed by the Angel Gabriel. According to their religious tenets, souls may migrate from body to body until they attain some kind of perfection, after which they no longer need to incarnate but join the world of eternal reality.

The Sufis of Syria, usually known as Druses, are strongly pro-reincarnation, while their other beliefs are an intriguing mixture of Islam, Judaism and Christianity. In Druse philosophy each individual is made up of soul, spirit and body; it is the union of these three elements − the body being by far the least important − which combine to make a human being. After death, the soul passes into any number of bodies, and each new person is independent of the last.

# Christianity

A mighty tussle has been fought by Christians on the subject of reincarnation. Although there are several references to rebirth in both the Old and New Testaments, many early Christians had great difficulty in accepting that Jesus, who was perfect, might be reincarnated in human form. Early Christians, and also Catholics today, accepted the idea of the assumption of the Virgin Mary straight into Heaven in some magical way. The idea that she, too, might be reincarnated was difficult to accept.

Despite these doubts, reincarnation remained part of Christian dogma until AD 553, when the Council of Constantinople decreed once and for all that it was a heretical doctrine, and that no Christian was to believe in it any more. It then became orthodox belief that souls did not have a pre-existence, but were formed along with the unborn baby, thence to be immortal. But after physical death, when souls might enter Heaven, Hell or purgatory, there was no more rebirth; once the body had died, Christian souls were forever united with God – or, in some cases, forever separated from him to spend the rest of eternity in Hell.

Two more Church assemblies, the Council of Lyons in 1274 and the Council of Florence in 1493, stated again that reincarnation was heresy and confirmed that departed souls would go to Heaven, purgatory or Hell. Anybody who dared to believe in reincarnation after this risked being condemned as a heretic, which meant death at the stake. The Inquisition effectively wiped out any remaining traces of a belief in reincarnation, and this non-belief has been a facet of Christianity until today.

But there was in fact a small sect of thirteenth-century Christians, living in the South of France and known as Cathars, who maintained a belief in reincarnation. To them, souls in bodies were actually fallen spirits who were learning important lessons through successive incarnations. Those who led good lives on earth might be rewarded by being reincarnated in bodies which would attain spiritual development.

The Cathar sect was completely annihilated by the Inquisition, who burned most of them at the stake. In the twentieth century, several people have had experiences and visions of past lives where they were burned at the stake. These past life Cathar experiences will be examined in Chapter 4.

Christianity therefore annihilated all traces of a belief in reincarnation, both by the proclamations of its various religious Councils and its habit of exterminating anybody who dared believe such a thing. The influence of Christianity also meant that many much older religions were all but wiped out – the pagan beliefs of old Norway, Ireland, Wales and England, and the ancient religion of witchcraft, or Wicca – (though there has been a modern revival: see Chapter 3). Again, the Christians had a habit of burning at the stake anybody who appeared to be a witch, or who held witch-like beliefs. No wonder most Christians came to believe that reincarnation was a primitive superstition and that no true believer in Christ could possibly countenance such an idea.

This state of affairs persisted in the West until the middle of the nineteenth century. True, there were occasional poets, writers and philosophers throughout the centuries who felt that rebirth was a distinct possibility, but they had little impact on the prevailing non-reincarnation ethic. Several of the Romantic poets, in particular Blake, Wordsworth and Coleridge, felt that reincarnation was possible. To the philosopher Voltaire, it did not seem at all odd that if a soul could inhabit one body, it might inhabit more than one, especially if it was supposed to be immortal. The French novelist Balzac became certain that reincarnation was experienced by everyone. In his novel *Seraphita*, completed in 1835, the heroine undergoes a long series of incarnations.

But it was only when religious persecution ceased in the West, and the way was opened for greater tolerance of a variety of beliefs, that the idea of reincarnation once more reared its head. It all began really with the founding of the modern spiritualist movement in the mid-nineteenth century. For several centuries Christianity had strongly discouraged any investigation into occult matters, but as it began to weaken its grip on society, interest in all aspects of the paranormal, or unexplained, began to revive.

## Spiritualism

Mediumship and spiritualism, as we understand them today, took root when groups of people on both sides of the Atlantic began to be convinced that it was possible to contact the spirits of dead people. Of course, interest in the paranormal had never really died out, but during the second half of the nineteenth century spiritualism became elevated almost to a religion in its own right.

It started, to all intents and purposes, when two American sisters, Margaret and Kate Fox, began to hear mysterious noises and raps in their house. Convinced that these noises came from spirits who wished to communicate, the sisters devised a kind of code whereby they could talk with the spirits. They elicited the information that the main communicator was a former inhabitant of their house who had been murdered and buried in the foundations. A search discovered some human remains in the foundations, but whether these were of the spirit communicator could not, of course, be established.

When the story of the Fox sisters was published in America it aroused a tidal wave of interest. Many other people, it seemed, had had experiences of communicating with spirits, and many more wished to do so. Within a very few years, huge numbers of spiritualist groups were founded all over America and Europe.

It did not die down when, later, Margaret Fox publicly retracted all her earlier claims, saying that the raps and other sound effects had been rigged by her and her sister to fool the grown-ups. Kate Fox joined her sister in denouncing spiritualism at a series of public meetings. But later still Margaret Fox renounced her renunciation, saying that the raps were genuine after all. By this time, though, spiritualism had gained a firm hold in the West and could not be dislodged by anything the Fox sisters had to say on the matter.

Spiritualists basically believe that the human spirit lives on after death, and that in many cases those still living on earth can contact these spirits to obtain wisdom and useful information. All spiritualist meetings take place with the aid of a medium, who supposedly can channel information from 'the other side' to those still living on this side.

Ever since spiritualism first became established, journalists and scientific investigators have looked closely to see whether there is anything in it or whether it is all a complete fraud. Very many of the mediums who have been investigated have been shown to be fraudulent, but that has not stopped large numbers of people believing that it is possible to contact those who are physically dead.

Spiritualism focused interest in the subject of mediumship, which is of course very much older, going back to ancient and tribal times. For the past 150 years sceptics have been asking themselves whether mediums really are in contact with some kind of spirit world, or whether their pronouncements come from deep in their own unconscious. Whatever the truth, there is no doubt that some people do possess extraordinary abilities to see and predict things which are not discernible through the five senses.

Many spiritualists would call themselves Christians, and certainly

Christian hymns are sung and passages from the Bible are read out at spiritualist churches. But orthodox Christianity has always frowned on spiritualism, believing it to be a dark and sinful practice. The point about the movement, which still flourishes all over the world, is that it brought the spirit world and that of physical reality closer together, and reinforced the belief of the ancients that physical existence is only a very temporary and relatively unimportant stage in the soul's passage to perfection.

Spiritualists are very divided on the reincarnation debate. Some, mainly those in France, accept rebirth as a reality, but most spiritualists in Britain and America seem to believe that we only inhabit a physical body once, and then return to the ethereal or subtle regions where we really belong.

The Society for Psychical Research, founded in 1882 by a group of Cambridge intellectuals, has always devoted much of its energies to investigating claims of mediumship. Although very many mediums have been exposed, there are some, such as Eileen Garrett, Ena Twigg, Ivy Northage and Edgar Cayce, who appear to have genuine powers, and whose pronouncements cannot easily be explained by any ordinary means.

# Theosophy

By far the most influential of the modern reincarnationist belief systems, theosophy was founded by Madame Helena Blavatsky, William Judge and Henry Olcott in New York City in 1875. The basic idea was to reconcile all world religions with a set of mutually acceptable ethical beliefs which were supposed to be founded on 'eternal verities'.

The leading light behind the movement, Madame Helena Blavatsky, was born Helena Petrovna von Hahn into an aristocratic Russian family in 1831. At seventeen she married Nikifor Blavatsky, more than twenty years her senior, but ran away after three months, and then, according to her own versions, travelled all over the world studying occult and mystical traditions. She was even supposed to have journeyed to Tibet, where she received instruction in remote monasteries. The system of beliefs she came to feel were true and universal were strongly influenced by Eastern religions. As such, her beliefs were to pave the way for the later acceptance of Eastern religions and philosophical ideas in the twentieth century.

It seems that HPB, as she liked to be known, had undoubted psychic gifts, and on landing in Cairo after a shipwreck she set up a spiritualist group. Two years later, aged forty-one, she sailed to New York which is where the theosophy movement began in earnest. At that time intellectuals and avant-garde thinkers were becoming profoundly interested in occult matters. One day HPB read an article on spiritualism, entitled *Astounding Wonders that Stagger Belief* by Henry Olcott, a former soldier. She decided she had to meet Olcott, and soon formed a partnership with him. Later they set up home together, but there does not appear to have been any kind of sexual relationship between them.

One of HPB's chronic problems was lack of money, and she soon found herself penniless. She decided that something 'quite out of the way must be invented' and suggested that she and Olcott should form a society dedicated to the study of occult beliefs and spiritualist practices. The new organization, which they called the Theosophical Society, did not catch on at first, but Olcott and HPB thought it might stand a better chance in India, where such beliefs were more readily accepted. As it turned out, theosophy became extremely popular in India. She and Olcott also founded a journal, *The Theosophist*.

Their new ideas caught the attention of the newly-founded Society for Psychical Research, whose members spent their time investigating so-called occult phenomena. As Madame Blavatsky was in the habit of receiving information through raps, chimes, ouija boards and other occult paraphernalia, she seemed a suitable subject. The investigator, Richard Hodgson, wrote of Madame Blavatsky in 1884: 'We regard her neither as the mouthpiece of hidden seers, nor as a mere vulgar adventuress: we think that she has achieved a title to permanent remembrance as one of the most accomplished, ingenious, and interesting imposters in history.'

However, this damning indictment did not stop the well-timed march of theosophy. There was no doubt that Christianity had been shaken to its roots by Darwinism, now beginning to be accepted by many thinking people all over the world. The Bible was wrong – the world had not been formed in seven days; nor had Adam and Eve been created specially by God. The resultant growing atheism and agnosticism among intellectuals of the day, however, left a definite spiritual gap: theosophy, which took on board many Eastern concepts, seemed an exotic and intriguing alternative. Few people then knew anything about comparative religion – apart from scholars, who kept their knowledge pretty much to themselves.

Theosophy shares a conviction with several of the ancient Eastern religions that those who love earthly pleasures and sensuous delights are reborn more quickly than people who aspire to higher things.

The two 'bibles' of theosophy are *Isis Unveiled* and *The Secret Doctrine*, supposedly written down by Madame Blavatsky under dictation from her Tibetan masters, or Mahatmas. Basically, theosophy holds that incarnation begins with mineral forms – which would appeal to the evolutionists – and progresses through to plant, animal, human and eventually divine forms. Once human consciousness has been attained, it never again reverts to animal form. This too would please the evolutionists, who were saying that humans evolved from a common ancestor with apes, but that the march of progress ensured that humans would never undergo a backwards evolutionary step to animals again. Blavatsky maintained that everything which has happened in the world was recorded somewhere in space on the so-called Akashic records; this idea later found an echo in Jung's exposition of the universal unconscious.

Theosophy took the idea of *karma* very seriously. It believed that *karma* was a law of absolute justice to which every being was subject. It was not divine punishment for sins, but worked completely independently of God. Humans were held to make their own *karma* here on earth.

Theosophy had a neat answer to the most common objection to reincarnation: if we have lived so many times before, why don't we remember anything of our past lives? The reason, according to theosophists, is that our past lives are largely irrelevant to the present one. The fact that we have no memories of them does not mean they haven't existed. After all, we have no memories of being a baby, or of being born – and yet we are in no doubt that it happened.

The main objection to theosophy has been that it is all so much guesswork and assertion. No proof or evidence whatever is provided for these beliefs, other than that they were dictated by perfect masters from the astral sphere. Nevertheless, theosophy caught the public imagination and is still in existence today. Whether its basic ideas came from Madame Blavatsky's fertile imagination or whether they really came from ancient masters can never be known. But in a way, that is beside the point. The whole movement, and the world-wide interest shown in it at the end of the nineteenth century, helped to familiarize people both with Eastern beliefs and with the idea of reincarnation. At the very worst, it made people think. And the concept of rebirth answered questions to which Christianity had no answers – those of why there is so much injustice and unfairness in the world today.

And the doctrine was not harmful in any way. Theosophy received an enormous boost in Britain when the remarkable Annie Besant decided to abandon her former atheistic beliefs and become a practising theosophist. Earlier she had enthusiastically fought for birth control, the Fabian movement and socialism; now she promoted theosophy with the same energy. The writers W. B. Yeats and Oscar Wilde became interested in the doctrines, and Yeats at least regarded Madame Blavatsky, who later settled in London and made her headquarters there, as genuinely psychic, even if she was given to trickery and cheating.

Annie Besant herself started communicating with astral guides and became the leader of the theosophical movement after HPB died in 1891. She went to India, where she was instrumental in picking a young, poverty-stricken Indian boy, Krishnamurti, to be the next Messiah. This beautiful child was taken over and educated by the theosophists, but at the age of thirty-four he formally repudiated their teachings and said publicly that he was not the new incarnation of Christ. Krishnamurti became a teacher of world renown in his own right.

Theosophy attracted a lot of interest at the time because its pronouncements – that it received wisdom from the starry spheres, that members had taken astral trips to Mars where there was intelligent life, and that spirit guides spoke to the leaders – made it fair game for newspaper investigation and exposure. The *Westminster Gazette* ran a long series of articles on theosophy, saying that if Madame Blavatsky's books had not been, as she asserted, dictated by the 'Mahatmas' (great souls) then the whole thing was so much rubbish.

# The Rosicrucians

One of a large number of reincarnationist orders that sprang into being after theosophy, the Rosicrucian movement, was founded in 1909 as a supposed revival of the Ancient Mystical Order Rosae Crucis. One of its basic beliefs was that we have to reincarnate again and again until perfection is reached, when we will be reborn no more but accepted by God for ever. According to the Rosicrucians, the average earth time between births was 144 years; nobody knows where this figure came from. The Society of the Inner Light, founded by the mystic and novelist Dion Fortune, who was active in the twenties and thirties, also maintained that the interval between death and rebirth was around 140 years. There seems no possible way of verifying this information, which Fortune took down from what he called the 'Inner Planes'.

# Anthroposophy

This belief system was founded by Rudolf Steiner, born in 1868 as an Austrian Roman Catholic. At an early age Steiner became interested in theosophy, and lectured with the Theosophists until Krishnamurti was declared to be the present-day incarnation of Christ. Since Steiner felt this could not possibly be so, from then on he distanced himself totally from the movement. However, theosophy had left its permanent mark. Steiner believed implicitly in reincarnation, and was apparently able to see into the past lives of people whom he met in everyday life. He later came to believe that all humans could possess this ability if they chose to develop it; for most, however, the ability to see people's past lives was buried deep in the subconscious.

According to Steiner, it was possible to investigate spiritual matters scientifically; this view paved the way for the scientific method to be used to evaluate spiritual matters – they did not, Steiner stated, have to be simply a matter of faith. He came to feel that scientific perception and psychic abilities could work together for the betterment of humanity – by building a much-needed bridge between the hitherto opposite disciplines of religion and science. He called this new science anthroposophy – 'anthropos' meaning man, and 'sophy' wisdom – and described it as 'a path of knowledge leading the spiritual in man to the spiritual in the universe.'

In 1913 Steiner founded the Anthroposophical Society in Switzerland. One of its major tenets was that reincarnation was an absolute fact, and Steiner believed that there was enormous evidence for such a belief to be found in the Bible.

He went on to found a number of schools all over Europe and the movement he founded is still flourishing today. Anthroposophy was suppressed by the Nazis, but after the Second World War it began to flourish again, and many hospitals and clinics dedicated to caring for the sick on anthroposophical principles were founded.

Steiner was a forerunner of the 'holistic' medical movement which has become so popular today. He believed that no medical cure can be effective unless doctors also address themselves to the spiritual aspect of patients. Anthroposophical medicine was founded on the belief that there are four distinct aspects to a human being, which must all be taken into account.

other physical things, including minerals; the life or 'etheric' principle, which we share with plants and animals; the sentient or 'astral' body, which we share with animals: and lastly the 'I', or consciousness, which is unique to humans.

A healthy life depends, Steiner said, on maintaining the correct balance between these four aspects. In humans, the most important aspect is the 'I', which is responsible for shaping individual destiny. Central to anthroposophical medicine is the belief that this 'I' continues throughout many incarnations, and that our current circumstances are the inevitable result of what we have done in past lives; we don't have to know what these past lives were to accept that our condition now is a direct consequence of what went before.

In order to treat illness successfully, a doctor has to understand this – to know what is the purpose of a particular illness and why it has befallen this individual. According to anthroposophical medicine we do not become ill simply because a part has unaccountably broken down, as with a machine: we have become ill because something in our past *karma* has to be worked out. An anthroposophically trained doctor will have received a formal medical training, but goes further than this: he will take not just a conventional history of the patient, but will look for underlying patterns to explain the present malaise. Treatment will depend on the individual's particular needs, and may consist of orthodox or alternative remedies. Steiner considered that successful therapy could include painting, drawing, sculpture, writing or developing any creative talent. Illness should be seen not as an unfortunate accident which has befallen a hapless individual, but a meaningful episode in his or her development from which there are important lessons to be learned. So the final aim of anthroposophical medicine is to facilitate lasting health, rather than relying merely on the improvement of symptoms.

Finally, Steiner believed that all humans have far greater potential than is generally realized. Modern life, however, he felt, does not usually allow latent talents to be developed.

# Edgar Cayce

Known as the 'sleeping prophet', Edgar Cayce was a true phenomenon whose life and work have made many previous sceptics rethink their ideas on reincarnation as a primitive superstition. Cayce (pronounced Casey) was born in 1877 in Kentucky and came from an uneducated farming background. After leaving school at fifteen, he worked as a photographer, clerk and insurance salesman. A fervent Christian from a fundamentalist background, he was for most of his life a Sunday School teacher.

After losing his voice at the age of twenty-one, Cayce allowed himself to be hypnotized, and the cure worked. He then discovered in himself an ability to go into trance, and it was in this state that his extraordinary abilities seemed to come out. Even though he had had little formal education, he appeared to have acquired a massive amount of knowledge on all subjects. When Cayce came out of his trance he could remember nothing of what he had said.

Another of his abilities was to lie down in a trance and make accurate diagnoses of sick people whom he had never seen or met. After a time, this 'paranormal' diagnosis became Cayce's main work, and he would diagnose and prescribe treatment for patients who lived hundreds of miles away. Again, when he came out of his trance he had no idea what he had been saying, or what medical terms he had been using.

This ability led to Cayce giving 'life readings' for people troubled by illness, anxiety or tension in their lives. Before very long, the past lives of some of these people would emerge and Cayce would comment on them. At first, delving into past lives caused Cayce enormous problems with his conscience, because as a committed Christian he was not supposed to believe in reincarnation; in the end, though, such a belief forced itself on him, although he remained a Sunday School teacher for the rest of his life.

Between 1923 and 1945 Cayce gave around 2500 life readings, all of which were supposed to show how previous lives intimately affect the present one. The life readings, which have all been carefully documented and preserved by the Edgar Cayce Foundation, give very definite information on how attitudes, personality traits and experiences are carried on from one life to the next. This happens even when we have no knowledge or perception of any past life – the experiences all count, and they all go to make what we are. Cayce came to believe that a large number of behavioural and psychological problems which had proved resistant to any kind of treatment were caused by the influences of past lives on the present incarnation.

Edgar Cayce eventually delved into his own past life and learned that he too had been through hundreds of incarnations. He also discovered, to his satisfaction, that many of his friends and family members had also been with him in past lives.

Since Cayce's death, his work has been subjected to an enormous amount of investigation. His son, Hugh Lynn, dedicated his life to furthering his father's work, and has made all the Cayce readings available for researchers. Of course, there have been the usual accusations of fraud, wishful thinking and fakery, but nobody has ever yet been able to offer a convincing alternative explanation for Cayce's ability.

There is no doubt that he did go into trance, there is no doubt that he was able to acquire astonishing amounts of knowledge while in an altered state of consciousness, and there is also no doubt that he diagnosed accurately the illnesses of hundreds of people whom he never knew. He made no money from his abilities, and for most of his life was relatively poor.

Edgar Cayce was very different from both Madame Helena Blavatsky and Lafayette Ron Hubbard, the founder of Scientology. Both these people were convinced from an early age that they were special – that they had some unusual function to perform in the world. Both of them either invented, or exaggerated, aspects of themselves to gain a cult following, and were extremely extravagant with the truth.

Whatever one's eventual conclusion on the reincarnation question, there seems no doubt that Edgar Cayce was absolutely genuine. His life was an open book and scholars are allowed to look freely through all his documented readings. The only mystery lies in his abilities, for which nobody has yet been able to provide a satisfactory answer.

# Scientology

Registered as a religion in America, scientology was founded in 1950 by the former science fiction writer Lafayette Ron Hubbard. It has often been condemned as a dangerous cult, but still survives and has many thousand adherents.

Scientology teaches that reincarnation is an absolutely inescapable aspect of the human condition. L. Ron Hubbard explains how it operates in his book *Have You Lived Before This Life?*, published in 1950 by the Church of Scientology of California, in which he defines scientology in typical grandiose terms: 'Scientology is an applied religious philosophy and technology resolving problems of the spirit, life and thought: discovered, developed and organised by L. Ron Hubbard as a result of his earlier

Dianetic discoveries. Coming from the Latin, *scio*, (knowing) and the Greek *logos* (study), Scientology means "knowing how to know", or "the study of wisdom".' (The word 'dianetics', also coined by Hubbard, comes from the Greek *dia* (through) and *noos* (soul); thus, 'though the soul' – a system for the analysis, control and development of human thought.) Scientology is absolutely steeped in jargon and very many terms connected with this belief system were made up by Hubbard.

As regards reincarnation, in the introduction to *Have You Lived Before This Life?* he says that, although reincarnation has mystified man, scientology can prove beyond all doubt that rebirth exists. 'The concept of reincarnation and Man's belief in the past and future continuum is as old as Man himself,' he states. 'It can be traced to the beginnings of thirty-one primitive cultures and has dominated almost every religion through history as a pivotal belief.'

Hubbard goes on to give a very brief history of the fortunes of this belief, saying that all early religions believed in reincarnation and the rebirth cycle, but that Christianity, in the sixth century, decided that it could not exist. Christians condemned the teachings of reincarnation as heresy, and it was at this time, says Hubbard, that references to it were expunged from the Bible.

The belief persisted in some circles in spite of terrible persecution, until it was rediscovered in the nineteenth century along with the subconscious and the new science of psychology. Freud and Jung acknowledged man's belief in his own immortality and reincarnation, Hubbard tells us, and adds: 'Their mistake was only in assigning this basic truth to imagination or fantasy.' But today, in scientology, Hubbard confidently asserts, 'the stigma of the subject has been erased and verification of past lives is fact'. The book goes on to detail a number of case histories of people (all anonymous) who have come to accept a belief in reincarnation through learning about scientology.

So, according to scientology, how does it all work? Again, Hubbard is completely clear on the subject, unlike those new to scientology, who are known as 'preclears' before they see the light. Hubbard explains it all neatly thus: human beings consist of two basic elements – the physical body and the 'thetan' (another scientology neologism). The thetan is the spirit which lives in the body and never dies. When physical death occurs, the thetan becomes separated from its body; and as soon as it realizes this it looks around for another suitable human body to inhabit. How do thetans behave when they haven't got a body? Hubbard answers:

They behave like people. They'll hang around people, they'll see somebody who's pregnant and they'll follow her down the street. Or they'll hang around the entrance to an accident ward and find some body that is all banged up and the being that had that body has taken off or is in a frame of mind to, and does so. He will pick up this body and pretend to be somebody's husband or something of the sort.

They [thetans] do all sorts of odd things. *When* a new body is picked up, *if* a new body is picked up at all, is not standardized beyond saying it usually occurs most of the time (unless the thetan got another idea) two or three minutes after the delivery of the child from the mother. A thetan usually picks it up about the time the baby takes its first gasp.

Would the body go on living without the thetan picking it up?

That is beside the point. It's a case of how fast can you pick one up before somebody else gets it. So there is a certain anxiety connected with this.

Another phenomenon of death, asserts Hubbard, is that a thetan will stay around a body until it is disposed of properly. He writes:

You can find times when he's been left out on a cliff and nobody even put the lid on the coffin. There it is exposed to the wind and rain and he'll stay around there until that body is totally dust.

Now, the rate of decay of a body is not really a point in question except a thetan will try to accelerate it if the body isn't cared for. A thetan doesn't much care concerning the actual disposition of the body as long as it isn't given any more indignity than it suffered in the lifetime. But he is apt to be very upset about indignities rendered to a dead body. He associates the body with his own identity to the degree that every time an indignity is rendered to the body he thinks it is to some degree being rendered to him. Therefore, he hangs around a body until it is properly disposed of.

So much nonsense – or divine wisdom? As with theosophy, scientology takes bits and pieces of Eastern religions and esoteric systems and moulds them into something seen as suitable for the modern person to accept. Also as with theosophy, the belief system relies on assertions and statements. No explanation is given of where these beliefs come from or why anybody should accept them as fact, and there is no indication of any evidence for these beliefs. Scientology tells us that it actually proves reincarnation – yet offers no kind of documentation for that proof.

However, both theosophy and scientology offer answers about the human condition that Christianity failed to provide. This is one reason why they have caught on – and by no means all adherents of either belief system are simple and uneducated. In both cases, people of considerable intellectual acumen and standing in the community have been attracted by the basic doctrines.

# The International Society for Krishna Consciousness

Adherents of the International Society for Krishna Consciousness are the so-called 'Hare Krishnas', instantly recognizable from their shaven heads and yellow robes as they process, chanting, down Western high streets. The Hare Krishna movement began in the West in 1969, and takes its inspiration from the *Bhagavad-Gita*. Its devotees are vegetarian and non-violent, and to them, Krishna is God.

This explanation of reincarnation by His Divine Grace A C Bhaktivedanta Swami Prabhupada, founder of the International Society, was quoted in Hayley Mills and Marcus MacLaine's book *My God*:

> When somebody dies, all that happens is that the spirit, the immortal part of humans, leaves the body. But although the body may be pronounced dead, the living force can never die. All through life, the body is changing. For instance, the body of a new-born baby is hardly the same as that of an eighty-year-old man. But the spirit stays exactly the same and is not influenced by bodily changes.
>
> When one body dies, the soul simply migrates to another suitable body. This spirit is invisible and has no material dimensions. Nevertheless it exists – in fact, there could be no

life at all without it. After the physical body is destroyed, the soul, or spirit, which is made up of the three elements of mind, intellect and ego, carries on. Nobody can see the process of transmigration of souls, but we can be sure that it is happening.

So how does it happen? According to Swami Prabhupada, the spirit soul enters into the womb of a potential mother through the semen of the father. The soul then goes on to develop a particular kind of body, which will not necessarily be a human one. A previous human soul may transmigrate into the body of a cat, a dog, even an insect. It all depends on what has been achieved – what kind of life has been lived previously. According to the International Society there are altogether over eight million different forms of life. A soul may enter into any one of them when the previous body has died. The thoughts we have at death are instrumental in determining what kind of body we may inhabit next.
  Swami Prabhupada says:

> If, out of ignorance, we commit sinful activities and violate
> nature's laws, we will be degraded to animal or plant life. Then,
> again, we must evolve by transmigration of the soul through
> various species to the human form; a process which may take
> millions of years. Therefore a human being must be responsible.
> We must take advantage of the rare opportunity of human life by
> understanding our relationship with God and acting accordingly
> in devotional service. Then we can get out of the cycle of birth
> and death in different forms of life.

In other words, the more 'spiritual' we are in our human lives, the less possibility there is that we may come back as an animal or plant in the next incarnation. One way of becoming spiritual, according to this movement, is to chant continually the names of God: Hare Krishna Hare Krishna Krishna Krishna Hare Hare Rama Hare Rama Rama Rama Hare Hare. This very practice, says the Swami, reminds us that our one true allegiance is to God. The more we can chant these words, the more likely we are to return in human form.

# The Brahma Kumaris World Spiritual University

Founded in the 1930s in India, this movement has now become a world-wide force for peace. It is affiliated to the United Nations, and holds regular conferences to promote world peace at its headquarters in Mount Abu, India, and around the world.

Adherents, who practise a form of meditation known as Raja Yoga, lead a strictly disciplined life, rising at four in the morning to meditate and attend a devotional class. They are strictly vegetarian and are also advised to be celibate. (In fact, very many of the modern Eastern movements recommend celibacy as a way of coming closer to God: the outstanding exception were the Orange People, or Rajneeshies, followers of Bhagwan Sree Rajneesh. However, since the AIDS crisis, these people too have been advised to embrace celibacy if they can – Bhagwan has pronounced that, if we are not very careful, AIDS, not a nuclear holocaust, will destroy the world.)

Unlike many Eastern movements, the Spiritual University does not recommend its members to withdraw from the world and retire into an ashram. Far from it – they are encouraged to keep their jobs, to go out into the world, and to show by example what a good life can be. It is one of the few Eastern-based spiritual movements to be run by women, although it was originally founded by a man.

To outsiders, the life may seem impossibly austere: members are recommended not to watch television, go to films or read books, in case these encourage 'waste thoughts'; they do not drink any alcohol or smoke cigarettes; and they will not usually eat food prepared by non-adherents, in case 'wrong vibrations' get into the dishes. The BKs believe strongly that negative thoughts and emotions can enter food and affect those who eat it.

The main reason for all these disciplines is so that members can cleanse their souls from the negative imprints of many previous births, and become perfect again. The idea is not to encourage any bad habits which could imprint themselves on the soul and lead to sorrow either in this incarnation or in successive ones.

I spoke to Sister Jayanti, director of the UK branch, for clarification on the BK philosophy of reincarnation and *karma*. Jayanti has been a member of the Brahma Kumaris for over twenty years and, although of Indian birth, was brought up and educated in the West.

She said: 'For us, reincarnation is inescapable from karma which in its literal translation means "action." Karma is simply the principle, observable throughout nature, that for every action there must be an equal and opposite reaction.

'In nature, the eternal question is always, which came first, the seed or the tree? For us, this indicates that there must be a cycle of rebirth. In nature, everything is cyclical – so why should humans be any different?

'To me, there are three possible explanations to the questions of why we are here and where we are going when we die. The first is that all human life is random and chaotic. Although life may seem like this to very many people, it is an unarguable fact that everything else in the universe follows a very definite pattern, whether you are talking about the seasons, about gravitational pull, about the movement of the planets. As everything in the universe without exception follows a pattern, why should humans, such an important part of it, be the exception?

'The second possibility is that whoever is the motivating force is merciless and unjust because it is evident that so much of human life is unfair. Yet every single religion portrays God as a benevolent being and teaches that goodness will always win in the end.

'The third possibility is that there is a law of cause and effect which operates beyond the one lifetime. In this birth one simply sees the effect of what has gone before. We may not know what these causes were, and in fact in most cases we don't know. But it seems logical that there must be causes whch are now triggering off the effect.'

If there is some kind of order in the universe and if there is some kind of cosmic justice, then all the good and bad which people have done in their lifetime should be settled before they die. 'Yet there is every indication that this doesn't happen,' Jayanti said. 'On the level of logic, it seems only fair that if I've done good in my lifetime I should reap the rewards. Similarly, if I've committed terrible sins they too should be accounted for in human terms. But in so many cases, the score is not anywhere near evened up at death.

'Christians hope and pray that if they are good they will go to Heaven and that bad people will go to Hell. But really, this is all in the realm of imagination and fantasy – it has to be an act of faith, because there has never been any evidence of any kind that we go to Heaven or Hell after death.'

Jayanti admits that reincarnation can never be conclusively proved one way or the other. 'There can never be any real evidence unless you believe people's accounts of past lives,' she said. 'And we can never be sure that they are not making them up. The way I see it is that in every aspect of the physical world, cause and effect applies. As humans are part of the physical world, it seems logical to accept that these universal laws apply to them.'

One objection often raised over reincarnation is that, if we do all have so many past lives, why don't more of us remember them? Why can they usually only be recalled – if at all – under hypnosis? Jayanti said: 'It's difficult enough to forget painful memories of the immediate past, so imagine how terrible it would be if we had to cope with dreadful memories from past lives as well. Life would be unbearable if everything from our past haunted and coloured the future. The way we see it is that the trauma of bodily death brings with it the mercy of forgetting our past life, so that there can be some kind of fresh start in this one.'

So how long is the interval between death and rebirth?

'Raja Yoga teaches that as soon as the soul leaves one body it will immediately enter another, except in very special circumstances where there is sudden or untimely death. In these cases, the soul suffers and wanders around the earth without a body for a time. This is what ghosts and apparitions are – bodiless souls who are still suffering the effects of the past birth.'

The next question, inevitably, was: what exactly is 'reborn'?

'We see the soul as basically a point of luminous energy', Jayanti said. 'It is non-dimensional and non-physical but within that point of energy are the aspects of mind, conscience and personality. These are all in a state of flux and change according to each rebirth. The soul can go up and down, be born in happy or sad circumstances, according to the conditions it has created for itself in the past birth.

'But the general trend is to move from high to low, which is why there are so many more poor, ill and unhappy people than rich, successful and happy ones. We believe it is only through special effort that one can reverse the downward trend, and that is the main reason for the various disciplines we follow. They are all designed to help the soul clear away the negative aspects of previous births and clean itself up, as it were.

'This is where *karma* comes in. The more wrong actions we do, the more the soul becomes accumulated with wrong thoughts, negative emotions, bad habits. But you can perform what we call pure *karma*, to make the next birth more fortunate. We differ radically from most other Eastern-based movements in that we believe there is only one specific period where the movement of the soul can be from low to high. In the world's history, this time is now – and is one reason, I'm sure, why so many more people are prepared to accept the idea of reincarnation than a century ago.

'As we see it, materialism grew and grew and came to a peak until most people were no longer in touch with the spiritual side of themselves. Then, sated with material things, there was a gradual change of direction, and a new awareness. The pendulum has started to swing in the other direction.'

Jayanti believes that the clearest indications for rebirth and *karma* can be seen by observing small children. 'The effects of past *karma* are seen very dramatically,' she said. 'However hard they try, no parents can guarantee for their children health, beauty, intelligence or success in relationships.

'Whenever a deformed or handicapped baby is born, people always ask: how could this happen to an innocent child through no fault of its own? The answer has got to be, because in the past this soul performed an action which has somehow created the deformity in the present life.

'Of course, doctors try to explain handicaps in terms of genes, and I don't deny that genes play a part. But then we have to ask: why was this child born to this mother? Why, out of four children, say, is only one handicapped?

'The next imponderable is beauty. Again, in a family you may get one beautiful child and the rest very plain. Why should this happen? To me, the only logical answer lies in past *karma*.

'We all know the ingredients which make a successful human being – health, beauty, intelligence, ability to form relationships, and to this I would add the ability to make money. Yet nothing parents can do can ever make these things happen.

'True, one can shorten the odds, but there is never any guarantee. It's the same with intelligence. Very simple people can give birth to a genius, and highly intelligent parents may have a simpleton. We all know of cases where this has happened, and it can't be explained in terms of genes.

'The ability to create money must also in our present society be seen as a blessing. Some children are born surrounded by wealth and continue thus, while others become extremely wealthy when they come from poor homes. We all know that it's not hard work which creates money, but innate abilities.' These aspects, said Jayanti, are all ingredients which indicate that other forces besides the genetic mix are at work.

Adherents of Raja Yoga do not believe that human souls can descend into those of animals. This is traditional Hindu teaching contained in ancient scriptures which she believes is a corruption of what was actually said.

'In the scriptures, there is talk of some humans having the consciousness of animals, the mind of a snake, a brain like a butterfly and so on, and it has been taken literally.

'But for us, descent into animal souls makes no kind of sense. It would be impossible for humans to repay past karmic debts while in the bodies of animals. Also, how ever would the soul rise back up to be human again? For instance, it may be regarded as a punishment for a human soul to be reincarnated into the body of a dung beetle. But for such a beetle to roll about in dung is pure ecstasy, so where's the punishment?'

'Also, in the thousands of case histories of people who have reported past lives, there has never been a single incidence of anybody remembering a previous incarnation as an animal.'

Many people objecting to the idea of reincarnation ask the question: if we are all reborn, and have had so many lives in the past, why are there so many more people around now than even twenty years ago?

'Raja Yoga offers an explanation of this,' Jayanti said. 'We believe that there is a bank of souls, a fixed number, and that these gradually enter human bodies as time goes on. There are always "new souls" coming down and this is why the population of the earth increases all the time.' Some reincarnationists teach that the soul enters the human body just after birth, others that it arrives with conception, but Raja Yogis believe that it enters the mother's body at around the fourth month, when the "quickening" is observed. Before that time, the embryo does not have a soul and is simply a piece of matter, a potential human being only.

'Many people find it hard to believe in reincarnation, particularly in the West, because of Christian teachings. My understanding is that Christianity in its original form allowed a belief in reincarnation, but an edict was issued in the fourth century AD telling people they must not believe in rebirth because it would affect the sale of indulgences. If one could go to a priest and buy an indulgence to have past sins forgiven, this would make the whole concept of rebirth redundant.

'Also, if there was rebirth, what would be the point of the crucifixion?'

Another difficulty is that many people imagine that a belief in rebirth has resulted in a fatalistic attitude to life, where one has no control over destiny.

'This idea comes about when *karma* is only imperfectly understood. We are saying, yes, what I am now is what my past has made me, but whatever I do in the present and future is creating my destiny. I can't do anything about what went before, but I can affect the future by my actions. This is why adherents of Raja Yoga have to make sure their actions are pure and positive, and do not create negative *karma* which will rebound into future lives, and also adversely affect the present.

'As I see it, the concept of *karma* seems such a simple and logical explanation of everything, and it doesn't permit any kind of superstition or blind faith. In the past, superstition has always been a tool used by the ruling classes to hold simple people back. And within the spiritual dimension, people have found it easy to divorce logic from belief. Raja Yoga encourages people to carry on their logic into the realm of spirituality – which was why it attracted me in the first place.'

## Siddha Yoga

Another of the Indian-based spiritual paths which came to the West in the Sixties, Siddha Yoga, was introduced into Britain and America by Swami Muktananda. The Swami was born in 1908 and began his spiritual journey at the age of fifteen; in 1947 he met Bhagwan Nityananda, of the ancient lineage of the Siddhis – enlightened beings. In 1961, when Nityananda died, or left the body, he passed the power of the Siddha lineage to Muktananda.

Siddha Yoga has become a big movement in the West and is a rich and powerful organization. It holds regular 'intensives' – two-day meditation retreats consisting of a mixture of long meditation sessions and talks by visiting swamis. Siddha Yogis are vegetarian and the strict ones rise at four to meditate. The tradition is basically Hindu and so Siddha Yogis believe that souls can go into any life form after death, including plants and animals.

In a book called *Does Death Really Exist?* Swami Muktananda, who died in 1982, outlined the Siddha Yoga position on death and reincarnation. To the Western mind, he said, death represents the ultimate failure and is a painful reminder of the limits of our capacity to control nature and destiny. With all our clever science, we have not succeeded in prolonging life much beyond the allotted three score years and ten.

But the Western view of death is a very limited one. The truth is that when we die, rebirth follows automatically, just as we buy new clothes to replace our old ones when they are worn out. A human being, said Muktananda, should realize that we are basically neither male nor female, but consciousness which can become free from all bodies, all pain, all pleasure. We are, whether we realize it or not, immortal, and the part of us which lives for ever is the important part. The only way we can free ourselves from our limited outlook is by constant spiritual practice, which will enable us to become aware of the divine spark within.

We fear death, said Muktananda, for no good reason. Even if we do fear death, we cannot escape it. It is also certain that we can take no wordly wealth or acquisitions with us. The only thing we can take with us when we leave our present bodies is an awareness of who we really are, which will intimately affect our next birth into a physical form.

Once we become aware that our actions have consequences which may reverberate for hundreds or thousands of years, Muktananda pointed out, we become much more conscious of what we do. If we do bad, wrong or immoral actions, we will inevitably reap the consequences. The circumstances of our present birth are determined by what we did before. After physical death, we may either ascend into Heaven or descend into Hell while awaiting our next birth. And make no mistake about it, Muktananda said, Hell is a reality – a place of utter filth and misery.

## Sai Baba

Famous in the West as the guru who can materialize gold watches and other precious objects out of nothing, Sai Baba has attracted many Western followers, some of whom have attempted to 'investigate' him to discover whether he is a consummate magician or really some kind of divine being. He is supposed to have about a million devotees altogether, around the world.

When Erlendur Haraldsson, an Icelandic psychology professor, went to India to study Sai Baba's claims, he was not allowed to investigate under 'laboratory conditions'. Nevertheless, Dr Haraldsson became convinced that Sai Baba really did possess magical powers, mainly because of his ability to materialize holy healing ash, or *vibuti*. But in his book describing the Sai Baba phenomenon, *Miracles Are My Visiting Cards*, Haraldsson does not offer any real conclusions. All he says is that he and his team had not been able to find any obvious fraud, and that Sai Baba could not have produced many of the objects by sleight of hand.

Sai Baba, now well into his sixties, is fond of telling devotees about his previous lives: in particular, he says he is another famous guru, Shirdi Baba, reborn. Many people have attested to his powers of clairvoyance, and his ability to see into the minds of his disciples. He is also supposed to make himself disappear, and to change the colour of his robe at will. Sai Baba does not, however, appear to offer any particular teachings on reincarnation, except to reiterate the traditional Hindu belief that human souls can migrate into other life forms after physical death.

# Nichiren Shoshu of the United Kingdom

This Buddhist movement has become extremely popular in the West during the 1980s, and its beliefs have attracted many celebrities and people in public life. It sounds new, but in fact the movement is centuries old, based on the teachings of Nichiren, a Japanese Buddhist who lived in the thirteenth century.

To this sect of Buddhists, God is simply the supreme vital force or creative energy which permeates the universe and is found in every human being. At physical death we pass into a period of latency, which is really neither existence nor non-existence but a kind of waiting time until we take another bodily incarnation. When the time is right we will take on a new physical form, and the same cycle of birth, growth and decline will happen again.

Richard Causton, General Director of the NSUK, says: 'Death is just an interval like a night's sleep, when, having cast off an ageing or increasingly inefficient physical form, we are born again and can continue our unique function in the pattern of life as a whole.'

We should never complain about our circumstances or feel bitter that we are not more beautiful, richer or more powerful, say Nichiren Shoshu Buddhists, because our present birth is the one which is exactly right for us. It will enable us to learn the lessons we need to understand before we can pass on to our next incarnation.

# Wicca or witchcraft

Witchcraft has often been called the oldest religion in the world, predating any formulated or supposedly revealed belief systems which are enshrined in written scriptures. But until 1953 in Britain it was difficult to be a practising witch, because witchcraft was outlawed.

Most of us retain a concept of witchcraft from the novels of writers like Dennis Wheatley, where it was very much tied up with Satanism and wickedness. But modern witchcraft, which in Britain really began with Alex Sanders in the 1960s, bears little relation to the Dennis Wheatley variety. Adherents of witchcraft, or Wicca, believe that all humans possess special or psychic powers which can be used to discover what will happen in the future. When the future is merely predicted, this is known as clairvoyance, but when these powers are used to try and affect the future, then it is seen as magic.

In common with most other religions, witchcraft accepts that there is both a physical and a non-physical realm. Vivianne Crowley, a psychologist and practising witch (but no relation to the infamous Aleister Crowley), writes in her book *Wicca*: 'Our time in physical incarnation is a gift from the Gods which is to be enjoyed and we should appreciate the joys of sensory experience of the world around us. However, we must also seek the spiritual growth which expands our consciousness and allows us to live on levels beyond the physical.'

Modern witchcraft definitely holds that there is a non-physical aspect of humans which lives on after bodily death, and most witches today believe in reincarnation as a fact. They also believe that initiation into Wicca is a kind of rebirth whereby the essential nature of the past personality is altered through a series of initiation ceremonies.

The question that is most often asked of practising witches is this: do the initiation rites and ceremonies really take place naked? The answer is, yes, they very often do take place naked. In some ancient mystery traditions, such as the Celtic, nudity was seen as offering some kind of supernatural protection. Nudity during initiation rites is also seen as a symbol of vulnerability, of placing oneself in the complete trust of others. 'It is as a child seeking entry into the world that we come to the edge of the circle for initiation,' writes Vivianne Crowley. The nudity aspect – which is not always followed in cold countries because of the weather – is an ultimate symbol of rebirth. We came into the world naked, and we come into witchcraft naked.

# The Occult

Although occult matters – dealing with spirits, spooks, ghosts and apparitions – go back to the beginnings of time, systematic study of occult matters only began a hundred years ago with the founding of the Society for Psychical Research. All through the nineteenth century there were claims from a number of people that they had contacted the dead, or that they had received guidance from spirits on the 'other side'. Were all their claims so much rubbish – or could evidence be amassed in a scientific, objective way for some kind of survival after death?

This was what the early – and indeed the present – psychical researchers wanted to find out. To the founders of the SPR there seemed to be two distinct types of possessed persons: the first was possessed against his or her will by some kind of malevolent discarnate entity intent only on doing harm; the second was voluntarily in touch with some kind of spirit which dispensed wisdom and charity and was entirely benevolent.

One of the early members of the SPR, Edmund Gurney, investigated hundreds of such cases and came to the conclusion that there was simply no explanation other than that of non-physical survival after death. Those who dismissed survival as total charlatanism and fakery, concluded Gurney, did so on evidence as flimsy as that which they try to dismiss. Professor Dodds, however, another early member of the SPR, asked in his pamphlet *Why I Do Not Believe in Survival* why, if spirits were so keen to contact the living, they only showed an inclination to do so after the start of the current spiritualist movement in 1848?

The answer to that of course, is that communication with the dead has been a widespread practice in many countries for thousands of years. The only reason spirits did not appear to contact British or European people was because Christianity outlawed the practice.

In his book *Mediumship and Survival*, parapsychology investigator Alan Gauld, a university lecturer in psychology, says that fraud and chance coincidence simply cannot explain the huge number of cases investigated by the SPR. On the question of reincarnation, Gauld reminds us that the recent growth of interest in Oriental thought has given Westerners a greater awareness of Eastern philosophies, which almost all accept rebirth.

Reincarnation, says Gauld, is clearly a form of survival, and evidence of reincarnation must also be evidence of survival. The ostensible evidence for reincarnation, Gauld states, ('ostensible' is one of the favourite words of SPR members – they do not like to be considered gullible) can be divided into two broad categories – the statements made by sensitives or mediums regarding the past incarnations of their clients, such as the Edgar Cayce readings, and the large number of cases of people claiming to have memories of previous incarnations. Claimed memories, according to

Gauld, can be subdivided into three further categories: first, evidence from hypnotic regression; second, ostensible recollection by unhypnotized adults of supposed previous incarnations; and third, children's ostensible memories.

Gauld comes to the conclusion that by no means all of the many cases on record can be put in the fraud or fakery category – there are simply too many of them, and in a large number of cases the subject has nothing whatever to gain by remembering a previous life. Many, he concludes, must fall into the 'not proven' category and be put in the 'pending' file.

Many spiritualists do not believe in reincarnation and state that the cases on record are far more likely to be instances of 'possession' by a discarnate spirit. In this case, the earthbound spirit of a disreputable person becomes in some way attached to a living human being and takes over their personality. Gauld, however, feels that a huge number of the reincarnation cases he has studied cannot possibly fall into this category. After examining the evidence, he concludes by saying:

> It is beginning to look very much as though, having begun by
> expressing my very considerable distaste for the idea of
> reincarnation, I have now, by eliminating all the possible
> alternatives, argued myself into a position where I am bound to
> accept it, or at any rate to begin a serious attempt to make sense
> of it. Can one indeed make sense of this or any other form of
> survival theory? If, after my death, some recently born young
> person starts to exhibit memories corresponding to my memories,
> skills corresponding to my skills, and so on, would it therefore
> follow that I am come again?

Most SPR researchers feel that there are simply too many cases of survival, reincarnation memories, examples of *déjà vu* and clairvoyance for them all to be completely dismissed. It seems most likely, according to present-day SPR researchers, that there is an aspect of humans which is distinct from the body and brain and which lives on in some form after death. As it seems to be mainly the memory which lives on, it must therefore follow, if survival is a fact, that the memory is not stored in the brain cells but belongs to some non-physical, imperishable entity.

In the past, the reality of apparitions, ghosts and discarnate entities of all kinds was accepted without question. In our more scientific age, we have tended to dismiss all this as primitive superstition. But it is a fact, says Alan

Gauld, that these days at least one in ten people will see a ghost, or have an out-of-the-body experience in which they will appear to leave their bodies and view the world from a different perspective. Because in present times we do not officially believe in ghosts, these experiences will often be explained away as hallucinations – figments of the imagination which have no external reality at all. In fact, most modern parapsychologists regard apparitions as simply hallucinations constructed by the mind of the beholder. The neurologist Oliver Sacks has collected a large number of such cases in his book *The Man Who Mistook His Wife for a Hat*; in all Sacks' cases, patients had something wrong with the wiring systems in their brains, and their hallucinations could be explained accordingly.

In another book, *The Mind of a Mnemonist*, Sacks traces the sad history of a man who could never forget anything, and whose mind was so burdened by memories that he could do nothing in the present. Again, there was a neurological explanation for his disability.

Alan Gauld writes that of the huge number of cases that the SPR has on record – some of which will be examined in the next chapter – by no means all can be explained in terms of neurological or brain disturbance. 'There is a sprinkling of cases,' he says, 'suggesting some evidence of survival.'

But, says Gauld, even if there is some non-physical survival after death, very many questions remain unanswered. Is there sentient survival, where we still have some idea of what is going on in the physical world? Do our personalities survive, or do they change when we pass over to the other side? Do we survive for only a short time after death after which gradual destruction of all memory and personality traces set in? If there is some kind of survival, is it enjoyable or horrible? Do we survive as separate individuals, or do we become dissolved in something much larger – a kind of universal unconscious?

Gauld concludes by saying that, a century ago, the SPR was run by wealthy individuals with private means and a lot of leisure time. He feels that we can never definitely establish the existence or otherwise of survival unless we can carry out far more research, and he laments the fact that, since grant-giving agencies have hardly enough money to tackle the problems in this world, they are hardly likely to subsidize and study problems relating to the next. He feels that, at present, a big act of faith is necessary to accept either the neuroscientific or the survival explanation of why some people seem to retain memories from the past, or see apparitions and ghosts.

As far as the SPR goes, all we know at present is that there is definitely something 'unexplained' about non-physical matters. The evidence cannot simply be dismissed, and yet people hesitate to say definitely, yes, there is such a thing as survival, and yes, we do live on in some form after death of the body and brain. Chapter 3 will examine how the so-called New Age Movement has brought many people closer to accepting the idea of reincarnation as a factual reality.

# CHAPTER THREE

## *The New Age and after*

### Twentieth-century rationalism

For most of this century, the numbers of people in the West who have taken the idea of reincarnation at all seriously has been extremely small. The few surveys that were carried out on the subject before about 1960 estimated that around 3 per cent of Europeans – no more – considered that reincarnation might be a possibility.

One major reason, of course, was that it was emphatically denied by the main religions influential in the West – Christianity and Judaism. A second reason was that the beginning of the twentieth century heralded the golden age of science, and from that time onwards educated people attempted to take a completely rational and objective view of everything.

People knew that, contrary to what the Bible said, the world could not have been created in seven days. Indeed, it had taken millions and millions of years to form itself. Jesus could not possibly have been born of a virgin, or have been the produce of a non-sexual union between a human female and a divine, non-physical being. Even if Jesus had been born of a virgin, He would have been She – the sex of a male child is determined by Y chromosomes, which are present only in sperm. The so-called 'miracles' in the Bible were patent nonsense: it was just not possible to turn water into wine, to walk on water, or to drive evil spirits out of people and transfer them to swine.

At the same time as science was trying to disprove all miracles and magic, the Society for Psychical Research was putting so-called paranormal phenomena to scientific scrutiny. It seemed that just about everything that was properly and objectively investigated – ectoplasm, spirit mediums, clairvoyance, levitation – was rapidly exposed as fraud and charlatanism. Under investigation, there appeared to be a rational, scientific explanation for everything that had previously been regarded as miraculous or spiritual. In the twenties and thirties, after the Society for Psychical Research had been operating for about fifty years, apparently no modern, intelligent person could believe there was a shred of truth in spirit visitations, mediumship, ouija boards, tarot cards, alien spacecraft or any other paraphernalia of the so-called 'unexplained'.

They could find no evidence whatever that there was a 'spiritual' or non-physical aspect of humans which continued to have some kind of life after death. Almost all of the leading scientists and mathematicians of the twentieth century pronounced themselves atheists and became certain in their own minds that there was no God, and that human beings did not possess any kind of immortal soul or non-physical component which either lived on after their death or was in existence before they were born. This life was all, scientists declared – and it was primitive superstition to believe otherwise.

While scientists were investigating and explaining the previously un-explainable, the new fields of psychiatry and psychology were gaining ground. In the past, those who were mentally ill had often been considered to be possessed by evil spirits, but new developments in psychiatry and new understanding of the workings of the mind showed this up as non-sense. Neurologists were able to demonstrate that in schizophrenia, for instance, certain essential connections were not being made in the brain. Depression could be a result of childhood experiences, current lifestyle, a bad diet or deprived environment. Psychopaths were people whose mothers had never loved them or who had experienced terrible deprivation as children.

Freud and other psychoanalysts showed that a large part of our memories, fears and neuroses were buried in the unconscious. The un-conscious mind, it was explained, was the largest part of the iceberg – the conscious mind was only the tip. It was only by tapping into the unconscious that long-held repressions and troubles could be released. Evil spirits? Nonsense.

And even in the things that could not easily be explained, such as where genius came from, or why children from the same family and born of the same parents were so often completely different from each other, we were confident that the new study of genetics would soon unlock the secrets. Surely the microscope and the telescope would eventually deliver all the secrets of the universe.

The drug revolution in medicine, which really got under way during the 1950s, meant that many mysterious diseases of the past – diseases which had once been considered a punishment for past misdeeds – became a thing of the past in a more literal sense. Vaccines enabled smallpox, polio, diptheria and many other afflictions to be completely controlled by medical intervention. The invention of mind-altering drugs such as the benzo-diazepine tranquillizers, lithium carbonate and sedatives enabled many previously 'mad' people to lead relatively normal lives.

As a result, the West became less and less interested in spiritual and religious matters – we soon began to feel that what couldn't be proved didn't much matter or wasn't very important; we were replacing old super-stitious beliefs with new certainties. Ever more people became disillusioned with orthodox Christianity, feeling that this religion was asking them to believe the patently unbelievable. And with the rise of feminism in the 1950s and 1960s Christianity, Judaism and Islam came to be seen as patriarchal religions which elevated men at the expense of women. It seemed to many feminists that the main purpose of religion was to do just that – to make men dominant and women submissive.

On the subject of life after death – where was the slightest shred of evidence? Nobody had ever come back to tell us what life was like 'on the other side' – unless you believed mediums and spiritualists, and only the credulous and gullible could do that. It seemed as if both Heaven and Hell were outdated, meaningless concepts which had no place in modern society. Those who wanted to be scientific and rational simply could not believe in that kind of thing. As religion gradually came to be written off, so did other apparently non-scientific concepts such as astrology, herbal medicine and healing fall into disrepute.

## A new search for spiritual values

Then, in the 1960s, arrived what has come to be known as the Age of Aquarius, or the New Age – an age of humanism, in which spiritual ideas were once again able to flourish. Suddenly, small groups of people all over the Western world were beginning to look again at some of the old ideas, and put them into a new context. A few people were starting to ask awkward questions about science and psychiatry. Were these subjects really so wonderful? There was still much that science could not explain, and psychiatry was certainly not able, as was once thought, to cure all the mentally sick.

There were still very many things that continued to be unexplained. In spite of being told they didn't exist, people continued to see ghosts. Although told repeatedly that they were all charlatans and frauds, people were continuing to contact mediums. People were still alleging they were able to get in touch with the dead. Some claimed to sight UFOs (Unidentified Flying Objects), or aliens. Even though scientists had long ago debunked astrology, large numbers of people were still taking notice of their 'stars' and were continuing to contact astrologers.

Then, all through the 1960s, large numbers of young people were beginning to feel that there must be more to life than a mortgage, a nuclear family, food in the fridge, a nine-to-five job, life insurance and a new car every two years. The late 1960s was the age of the hippies, the counter-culture, of making love not war, when many of the values of the previous generation were being called into serious question. The young people in many countries of the Western world in the 1960s were the first generation to be able to enjoy enough food, warm homes, material plenty, a good education and free medical care. They were the first generation ever to be offered practically foolproof contraception and thus to experience sexual relationships without the consequences of unwanted pregnancy. And yet all this plenty, all this freedom, was not enough. There remained the feeling that there must be more to life, and many people were feeling empty inside.

Yet a return to orthodox religion was not the answer. Established religions were too condemnatory, too insistent on sin and guilt, too steeped in the past, in politics, patriarchy, bloodshed and wars. Something new was needed. The first young people who went on what came to be called the 'hippy trail' to the Himalayas found to their surprise that several of the very ancient religions, such as Hinduism and Buddhism, held answers to their questions, and could explain the meaning of life in terms that made more sense than narrow Christianity or Judaism. And at the same time as large groups of Westerners were discovering India and the Far East, a number of Eastern gurus, or holy men, began to arrive in the West with new messages of hope, love and peace. Before long Eastern-based ideas such as transcendental meditation, Siddha Yoga, Raja Yoga, Krishna Consciousness and Zen Buddhism, began to gain a foothold in the West, in spite of being almost universally condemned by orthodox Christianity.

Several Eastern gurus, such as Sai Baba who claimed to be able to make watches and other precious objects materialize out of apparently nothing, began to make an impact in the West. Two in particular, Bhagwan Sree Rajneesh and Swami Muktananda, became very influential, rich and famous, driving round in limousines and wearing expensive robes. They collected ever more Western devotees, who hung on their every word. When the Beatles, the most feted pop group ever, embraced transcendental meditation, the influence of Eastern cults and sects had to be universally acknowledged. And central to all these groups was a belief in reincarnation as absolute fact.

## Science opens its mind

As modern, Westernized versions of Eastern beliefs began making inroads, events were taking place in science and technology which were calling the rational, materialistic approach into question. In 1966, for instance, men landed on the moon, and although this in itself had little to do with reincarnation it started to open up people's minds to the possibility of space travel, and to give a more cosmic view of life.

Then the so-called 'new physicists' began telling us that what we had assumed was solid matter might not be all that solid after all, but might consist of particles in a constant state of flux. They were also telling us that there was no such thing as rational, objective fact – universal laws which were obeyed whether humans were there or not.

They were saying quite the opposite, in fact – that there was no such thing as absolute objective reality, but that all depended on the viewpoint and perspective of the observer. What had been accepted and revered as scientific fact might be, in fact, only interim theory – something to keep us going until new knowledge was gained.

Then books began to be written which tied up new developments in physics with ancient beliefs in the spirit, in cosmic justice. These writers were discovering that ancient and modern truth had very much in common, after all, and were far less at variance than had once been thought. The ancients might have known something, after all.

The repeal of the Witchcraft Act in 1953 in Britain also had far-reaching effects. It paved the way for ancient religions, or paganism, to flourish again. At the very heart of paganism was a belief in reincarnation.

## The failure of medicine and psychiatry

Meanwhile, things were also happening in the medical and psychiatric spheres. By the mid-1970s we were beginning to realize that the so-called drugs revolution, which promised to deliver a magic bullet for every disease, a pill for every ill, was not working out at all as expected. Many of the chemicals hailed as miracle drugs were found to produce side-effects that were sometimes far worse than the original disease or condition. Thalidomide is a notorious example.

We were very quickly learning too, that psychiatry didn't hold all the answers. In spite of our new knowledge about the unconscious mind, about childhood influences, about repressions and neuroses, people were still becoming and remaining mentally ill. Psychiatric treatments seemed unable to touch many deep-seated fears and problems: they could not touch depression and schizophrenia; they could not predict psychopaths or homicidal maniacs; they could rarely help young women suffering from eating disorders, hyperactive children and women who suffered post-natal depression. There were no successful treatments for drug addicts, alcoholics, gamblers and others gripped by destructive compulsions. All that psychiatrists could do, it seemed, was to hand out stronger drugs than the GPs could prescribe.

## The search for alternatives

The upshot of all this was that people began to wonder once again whether there might be more to human beings than an admittedly complex arrangement of nerves, bones, flesh, hormones and genes. Maybe there was, after all, some aspect of human life which could not be measured or analysed by science, but which nevertheless has a profound influence on behaviour, thoughts, concepts and relationships.

And so, throughout the 1960s and 1970s, little by little the way was paved for new versions of old beliefs to be considered. Mediums and psychics, who had so recently been completely discredited by men – and they almost all were men – of science – once more began to flourish. Those who claimed some kind of sixth sense, or paranormal ability, were once more held in some regard. Millions of people watched Uri Geller bend spoons on television in the early 1970s, and asked themselves: does he possess genuine paranormal abilities, or is he simply a super-clever magician? People tried to discredit Geller, but confusion remained. The confusion was heightened when, after watching Geller on television, children began bending spoons and twisting metal quite easily: several of them seemed to possess the ability to do what was scientifically impossible.

Some of these children were investigated under laboratory conditions by Professor John Hasted at Birkbeck College, London University; he discovered, much to his own astonishment, that some children really did have this 'psychic' ability. Psychologist Dr Ernesto Spinelli conducted an experiment in which primary schoolchildren were asked to guess which pictures were on the other side of a screen. Their answers came out far higher than chance.

Once again, those claiming paranormal abilities or experiences were investigated seriously. Ghosts and poltergeists were less readily dismissed. The case of Matthew Manning, who experienced strange poltergeist activity round him as a schoolboy, aroused enormous interest. There seemed to be something about these cases which defied standard rational explanation. Now, also, those claiming psychic abilities began to attract huge crowds. Mediums like Doris Stokes and Doris Collins attracted huge followings whenever they held public meetings, and it was necessary to book weeks in advance to attend one of Ena Twigg's meetings. When Doris Stokes' fame was at its height, the *Sun* newspaper, with its circulation of over four million, retained her as its resident medium. When a rival newspaper, the *Daily Mirror*, said that the *Sun*'s extreme right-wing views were worse than Hermann Goering's, Doris was asked to get an interview with Goering – wherever he might be. She obligingly dug up his spirit from somewhere and Goering said that in his opinion the *Sun* was an extremely good newspaper; he added that it was 'jolly hot down here'. When Doris Stokes died the *Sun* immediately announced that they would get the first interview 'from the other side'.

All fun and nonsense, not to be taken seriously? Perhaps. The point is, though, that the paranormal is now paraded daily in the world's best-selling daily newspaper, which gives some indication of the level of interest in the subject. The editor and staff might be cynical, but they know that their readers lap it up. Ten years ago, an equally cynical editor and staff would have known that their readers would not lap it up – the whole subject was at too low an ebb even to be mentioned.

Another popular British newspaper, the *Sunday Sport*, started off life by being just another downmarket tits-'n-bums rag. But it soon tapped another subject of abiding interest, and also a completely new market, by concentrating on the paranormal. Stories such as 'Hitler was an alien' have now become present-day clichés. The editor of this newspaper discovered, quite by accident, that the public had a seemingly insatiable appetite for stories about ghosts, aliens, reincarnation experiences and other 'weird' subjects. The *Sunday Sport*, aimed originally at the most downmarket readership there was, has found a new readership in yuppies, university students and the intelligent middle class. These readers purport to laugh at the contents, but a small voice inside them keeps asking: is there, could there be, at least something in it all? And of course in America the *National Enquirer*, the *Star* and their many imitators have for a long time known that there is a huge market for stories about the unexplained.

## Healing and astrology

As conventional medicine was increasingly seen to be, if not a completely naked emperor, at least an emperor with far fewer and poorer clothes than had once been thought, new kinds of healers began to spring up. The National Federation of Spiritual Healers was formed, and helped to bring back the art, rather than the science, of healing. The most successful healers were often men and women without any formal medical qualifications at all. At first the public was suspicious, wondering if these new healers were just old charlatans in a different guise, until it was realized that some of these people had remarkable successes by addressing the spirit, rather than the body, of ill people.

Even astrology, that ancient art so contemptuously dismissed by scientists and popular astronomers such as Patrick Moore, was becoming respectable once more. Scientific research throughout the 1960s had seemed to indicate that there might, after all, be 'something in it'.

# The revival of interest in reincarnation

In view of this ever-growing interest in spiritual and paranormal matters, in 1980 Gallup Poll commissioned a nationwide survey into the views of Americans on life after death. They found that, overall, 23 per cent of Americans now believed in reincarnation. A previous Gallup Poll survey undertaken on the same subject in the UK in 1968 had found that only 18 per cent of people accepted the idea of reincarnation; a further UK survey in 1979 showed that this had now shot up to 28 per cent. The highest number of believers were in the twenty-five to thirty-four age group.

Since 1980, when the last major survey was undertaken, there has been more interest in reincarnation than ever before. The Eastern-based movements of the 1960s have not gone away but are becoming ever more respectable and are attracting ever larger numbers of people. The earliest devotees were often hippies, rootless people, those without a place in society. Now, though, Eastern movements are attracting people from the world of showbiz, politics, medicine and science. A new type of medium or channel, claiming to be in contact with discarnate entities and preaching messages of universal love, harmony and wholeness, has become extremely popular in America. People with medically incurable problems such as phobias and psychosomatic diseases are now flocking to alternative healers, who often probe into their past lives to try and gain an explanation of present problems.

The subject of reincarnation has received its biggest boost from the film star Shirley MacLaine, who has now written a number of books on her own experiences in this area. She firmly believes that our spirits are truly immortal and take many incarnations into different physical bodies.

In 1988 British actress Hayley Mills, herself a follower of the Hare Krishna movement, published a book of letters from the famous about God. Called *My God* and co-authored with fellow Hare Krishna devotee Marcus MacLaine (no relation to Shirley), the book asked a variety of people in the public eye whether they believed in God and what they considered happened when they died. It was a revelation. Just about all of the younger people who gave their views revealed their belief that we come back in some form after we die, and that we possess a spirit – something non-physical.

The book attracted massive interest and its contents became front-page stories in many British newspapers. Neither Hayley Mills nor Marcus MacLaine was afraid of saying to cynical interviewers from the press or TV that they believed reincarnation to be an absolute fact; they believe that we may be reincarnated as animals, or even insects. A few years ago people would have laughed to hear a celebrity seriously saying such things. Not today. Clearly some aspects of the New Age movement have awakened a massive interest in subjects once thought to be dead and buried and parcelled away for ever; and the new interest is forcing people to re-examine their beliefs about reincarnation.

## Mediums and channels

Ever since the beginning of time there have been people who purported to be able to foretell the future or impart great wisdom by getting in touch with discarnate or disembodied spirits. And always, the subject has aroused great fascination and awe. At certain times in history, those who claimed to be in touch with physically dead entities have been held in honour and respect, while at others they have been ridiculed or have risked being exposed as fakes.

In our own supposedly rational age, one of the problems has been putting such people to any kind of objective test. It is impossible to prove that they do contact spirits. On the other hand, nobody can say with total certainty that they don't. Ever since mediums and psychics began to be scientifically investigated about a hundred years ago, it has been noticed that they often go into a kind of trance – that there is some kind of altered consciousness and that sometimes an 'entity' seems to take them over completely. In certain cases it has been observed that the medium imparts knowledge that could not possibly have been known by ordinary means. On the other hand, many people have been disappointed when visiting a medium supposedly in contact with a wise spirit because they have only received banal platitudes. One explanation often offered for the disappointment is that mediums, like any other group of people, vary enormously in their abilities and some are very much better than others.

All throughout the 1920s and 1930s there were mediums working in America, Britain and the rest of Europe. They had their followers, but on the whole they were very much underground and working in secret. Famous names of the time included Alice Bailey, who became a channel for an entity she called 'The Tibetan'. She claimed to write down everything just as 'The Tibetan' dictated, and her books are full of occult, astral and cosmological matters. Another English channel, who went under the pseudonym of Dion Fortune, claimed that one of her books, *The Cosmic Doctrine*, was received by the 'Inner Planes' during 1923 and 1924. The entity who dictated the words was, she said, somebody who had become a world-famous philosopher and teacher in his last incarnation, and was now, in the spirit world, one of the 'Greater Masters'. Unfortunately, the 'channelled' literature of both Alice Bailey and Dion Fortune is virtually unreadable. It is full of intimations that the cosmic world is full of love, peace and harmony and that down here we must live in universal brotherhood. Unfortunately, the supposed spirit guides seemed unable to communicate in plain English.

One 'spirit guide' for a group of British mediums meeting in the 1930s was known as 'Silver Birch'. The group centred round a popular newspaper journalist of the time, Hannen Swaffer, and was known as Hannen Swaffer's Home Circle. The best-known medium in this circle was Maurice Barbanell, the founder and first editor of *Psychic News*, which is still going today. These mediums had their loyal followers, but were not much believed in or taken notice of by the general public, and certainly had very little credibility – they were ridiculed in novels of the time by authors such as Graham Greene.

Then along came somebody who seemed to be different from the rest, to have actual powers of divination, and to say things which could be checked out – Edgar Cayce, who was mentioned in Chapter 1.

Cayce was the first 'trance medium' whose words have been systematically catalogued and analysed, and the thirty thousand or more readings that he gave in his lifetime are available for anybody to see at the Association for Research and Enlightenment at Virginia Beach in the USA. Cayce claimed that no discarnate spirits visited him, but that when in trance he was able to tap into some kind of universal unconscious. Whatever the source of his revelations, his many books on the subject became extremely popular and have sold millions of copies.

After he died in 1945, Jess Stearn was commissioned to write his biography. She went to a medium, Madame Bathsheba, who got in touch with Cayce. He told her that he would be guiding her hand as she wrote. The book was written in just a few weeks, and Stearn went on to claim that Cayce more or less dictated the book from 'the other side'. Even the title, *The Sleeping Prophet*, was provided by Cayce, she said. Whatever the truth, this book too has sold millions of copies.

Most of today's mediums would say that Edgar Cayce ushered in the modern age of channelling. Now, in America at least, it has become a huge industry with modern, or present-day, channels and mediums churning out books which they claim to have been dictated by the disembodied entity which has, for some reason, attached itself to them. Usually the books produced under such influences have a prophetic tone, and they all say much the same thing – that we should be aware of cosmic harmony, should strive for love between humans, and should not be narrow in our aims and ambitions but look to cosmic matters. Most 'channelled' books predict that a new age of love, peace and harmony is just round the corner. Recent major American channels include Ruth Montgomery, whose books – with titles such as *Born to Heal, Here and Hereafter* and *A Search for the Truth* – have sold millions of copies; Ruth Norman, who has produced at least sixty volumes of 'channelled' material; and perhaps the best known of all, Jane Roberts, who claimed she was a trance channel for the discarnate entity known as 'Seth'.

It all began for Jane Roberts in September 1963, when she was thirty-four. She became overwhelmed by the conviction that something from another reality, or dimension, was trying to contact her. She told her husband about it, and both of them began to experiment with a ouija board. Soon, somebody came through who first identified himself as 'Frank Withers' but who soon said that he preferred to be called Seth, and described himself as 'an energy personality essence no longer focussed in physical reality'. Jane Roberts was to channel Seth for the next twenty years, until her death in 1984, and was eventually able to amass a huge body of literature supposedly coming from this entity. The books are revelational in tone and intellectually demanding. They are certainly not aimed at those with below-average IQs, although they have been denounced as complete rubbish by several American sceptics who have studied them closely.

Jane Roberts also later said that she was able to channel two other sources: the painter Paul Cézanne and the American psychologist William James, father of the novelist Henry James. It is the information channelled through Seth, however, that has struck at the hearts and minds of thousands of Americans, including Shirley MacLaine. Seth's main message appears to be that each of us creates our own reality, by our beliefs and desires. Reality can change and be transformed, not just by our experiences, but by the interpretation we put on them, and by our readiness to be open-minded about things which cannot be explained or experienced through the five physical senses.

Since Jane Roberts, other American channels have also become famous. The best known of the current crop are J Z Knight, Kevin Ryerson and Jach Pursel. Knight, a former TV producer, claims to be able to channel 'Ramtha', an entity who was last in physical form thirty-five thousand years ago. Ramtha, like Seth, says that we all create our own reality, and mentions cataclysmic changes which are just around the corner for us earthlings. Kevin Ryerson, for whom the reality of reincarnation is a popular theme, seems to have several spirits who speak through him. One of his main entities is prosaically called John, and is a member of the Essene Hebrew sect who lived at the time of Christ. Shirley MacLaine has great respect for Ryerson, whom she calls 'one of the telephones of my life'. Jach Pursel, a former insurance supervisor, found that he contacted an entity known as 'Lazaris' when he attempted to meditate. Lazaris, who has been coming through Pursel since 1974, says much the same as Seth and Ramtha – namely, that we are all evolving, spiritual, immortal beings at one with the universe, but we must work hard to overcome negative tendencies within ourselves. Lazaris states, through Pursel, that he is not a dis-embodied entity as such, as he has never been physical or human, but is a 'group being living in another dimension from ours where space and time as we know it do not exist'.

All these three present-day channels have appeared on many American television and radio programmes, and have had continual exposure to the media. Unlike many mediums and channels of the past, they have no desire to keep their information limited to a few scattered believers; they are after the widest possible audience via the mass media. They are ready for any questions, as is Shirley MacLaine – they feel they have nothing to hide.

The big questions remain: are these channels genuine? Are they really in touch with discarnate entities from another, or higher, reality, or is it all just a giant confidence trick, of entertainment value only? There is no doubt that the channels in vogue at the moment are earning huge sums of money, and all of them are extremely rich. Most channels in the past did not amass any personal wealth, and were usually rather poor. It is also worth bearing in mind the prophetic saying of L. Ron Hubbard, the founder of scien-tology: if anybody wants to be rich, they should found a new religion. And this is in effect what the modern channels are doing – they have a completely new message of peace and love and hope which cannot be read about in orthodox religious literature. Also, at the very least, they are fun. They provide something for us to think about, and even to be hostile about and reject. They are sparks of something different in a world which for most people is extremely mundane.

At the moment, nobody has any conclusive proof either way. All that can be said at this stage is that the channels who have acquired fame and fortune genuinely believe in themselves, and there seems to be nothing harmful or 'evil' in anything they are saying. On the contrary, they appear to be doing a lot of good, and offering hope and comfort to large numbers of people.

In Britain there are no such luminaries. British psychics seem, on the whole, to be far quieter and more low-key in their pronouncements. Even the late Doris Stokes, who became a household word during the 1980s, never had the glamour and razzmatazz of the American channels. Even so, Doris was taken seriously enough for her claims and alleged powers to be put to the test by American James Randi, who goes around exposing fraudulent mediums and channels. The results of his Stokes investigations were published in a series in the *Sunday Times*. Randi felt that little of what Doris said was of much significance or was beyond all doubt from the spirit world. The information was very often vague and inconclusive and, in several cases, quite wrong. Doris Stokes and her successor, Doris Collins, never channelled specific entities, but even so they would consider themselves channels for disembodied spirits.

At the College of Psychic Studies in London, ordinary people can go on courses to learn how to become psychic, to tap into the spirit world. Several of the author's friends and professional acquaintances have been on these courses, for a variety of reasons: some have had unusual experiences which they believe might be extra-sensory, while others would like to be able to get in touch with those who have 'passed over' – the novelist Rosamund Lehmann, president of the College of Psychic Studies, became interested in such matters when her beloved daughter died. Yet others are simply interested in seeing whether they have psychic abilities, whether they could become healers, or whether they can get to the bottom of the mystery.

At both the College of Psychic Studies and the Spiritualist Association of Great Britain (SAGB) they keep an open mind on the subject of reincarnation. Both bodies are in no doubt at all that our spirits enter another plane when we die, and that in some cases they can communicate with those still on earth. Both organizations believe that, once it sheds its physical overcoat, the spirit becomes more refined, wiser, more divine in nature. Some spiritualists believe that everybody reincarnates at some point, while others say that only some people take new bodies once the old one has died.

Most spiritualists believe that certain spirits remain earthbound – that is, they are too animal-like or degraded in nature to ascend to the astral spheres. It is these earthbound spirits which do mischief, and which turn up as ghosts, poltergeists and even evil spirits which do harm.

The SAGB has a very rigid code of practice for anybody who wishes to become a medium. The aspiring medium has to be tested under laboratory-like conditions, and the information received 'from the spirits' must be able to be checked out objectively. Otherwise the person is not sanctioned by the SAGB, although of course there is nothing to stop them practising if they want to. Both the SAGB and the College work hard to stamp out fraudulent practices and to give mediumship and psychic abilities as credible an image as possible. Certainly all their public meetings are always packed, and there is currently a very long waiting list at either place for anybody wishing to see a medium or 'sensitive' as these people are known. Both organizations deplore those who wish to make money out of mediumship, and their charges per hour are very low indeed. Some mediums, indeed, do not charge at all, but rely completely on voluntary donations. Such people take the attitude that they cannot charge for information which is simply channelled through them.

What does all this tell us about reincarnation? Certainly, channels, mediums and sensitives provide no proof for those who are looking to be convinced. But their very popularity gives an indication of how much interest there is in the subject, and how ready we all are to listen to what these people have to say. Perhaps underneath the apparent scepticism there is a little, irrational feeling that there may be something in it – and that there may be a 'higher', or at least, other, reality than that mediated through the five senses.

If we can accept the notion that something of us is left after death, some-thing important and evolving, then it can only be a short step towards believing, logically, that the 'something' could incarnate into another human body. For after all, if the soul, as Christianity tells us, is immortal, then logically it can have neither beginning nor ending.

The main message that all the psychics, mediums, channellers and sensitives are revealing is that each of us is wonderful, unique, immortal, talented, wise, clever, a divine being – but that we may not have realized it. It is a message of total positivity, whether it comes from the starry spheres, the depths of the medium's unconscious, from books that have been read, or from the fact that most mediums are extremely canny psycho-logists. But perhaps it all adds authority if the message is coming not from

Jane Roberts, ordinary housewife, but from an astral entity called Seth, who has never been human.

# Astrology

There has always been a strong connection between astrology and the concept of rebirth. Those who wish to dismiss astrology, however, will find no difficulty in doing so. Cynics will say that it comes from a time when people had a very different concept of the universe from the one that we have now. Now extremely popular, astrology was virtually unknown in the West until the advent of theosophy, when Madame Blavatsky and, later, Annie Besant proclaimed that the planets did have a direct influence on our personality and behaviour. The theosophist doctrine on astrology had come, of course, from its intimate connection with Eastern religions, which take astrology seriously. Of course in the East astrology is inseparable from reincarnation; in the West some astrologers take the concept seriously, while others feel it goes against their basically Christian background.

American writer and TV personality Henry Gordon, who delights in debunking every aspect he can of the New Age movement, says in his book *Channeling into the New Age*:

> The fact that astrology derives its roots from an era when the earth was considered to be the center of the universe, and is therefore based on a foundation of false premises, has made little difference in recent centuries. It has gone through several cycles of popularity over the ages. With the advent of channeling, crystals, and all the other trappings of the New Age, astrology appeared to be going into one of its somnolent periods. But the publicity generated by the latest flap [the revelations that Nancy Reagan has employed an astrologer] has caused the rubber duck to surface yet again.

Gordon goes on to say that it really should come as no surprise that Ronald Reagan has indulged in occult practices, as astrologers hundreds of years ago catered exclusively to kings, queens and emperors. He adds that it has only been in modern times – this century – that commoners have been allowed to benefit from the 'doubtful and dubious delights dished out by the dispensers of cosmic wisdom'. Gordon has a nice turn in alliteration, well in keeping with his debunking pronouncements.

As with the various channellers and psychics, nobody can ever know for sure whether there is anything in astrology, whether all astrologers are making it up, consulting meaningless charts, or whether they are tapping into some similar cosmic wisdom that the channels claim to receive. It is, however, a fact that many more papers and magazines than ever before now carry astrology columns. It is also a fact that many businesses and commercial concerns rely on, or at least use, astrologers when recruiting staff or when trying to discover whether the time is right for a takeover, to expand or to retrench.

Astrology, basically, is the belief that there is a connection between the positions of the sun, moon and planets and the personality, behaviour and spiritual development of human beings. For many centuries astrologers have believed – and still believe – that the moment of birth, down to the exact hour, is extremely significant and affects personality in very dramatic ways. In some countries, notably India, it is still the practice that every new-born child will have a horoscope drawn up. When the time comes for the arranged marriage – and this may be done when the child is still a child – the horoscope will be consulted to see whether the intended partner is suitable. If not, that marriage will not be arranged.

For most of this century scientists have taken it as axiomatic that astrology was so much superstition, suitable only for primitive peoples. The majority of educated people accepted this, and astrology fell into serious disrepute. Then, in 1969 – just when the New Age was well under way – a French psychologist and statistician named Gauquelin, at the Psycho-physiological Laboratory in Strasbourg, decided to put it to a modern test. Himself thoroughly believing that astrology was so much nonsense, he took a sample of the birth dates of six hundred members of the French Academy of Medicine. If there was anything in astrology these people should show something in common, as they were all doctors. He found, to his surprise, that a higher proportion than just chance had been born when Mars and Saturn were in significant positions.

Believing that this might be chance, Gauquelin took a further sample of five hundred doctors and was astonished to get a similar result. Later studies on the same subject showed that a high proportion of athletes, politicians and military leaders shared certain planetary aspects at birth. Further work in America confirmed Gauquelin's work. In Britain, the former professor of psychiatry at the Institute of Psychiatry, Hans Eysenck, tested out Gauquelin's findings – and pronounced them correct. The sceptics were flabbergasted. A few years later, the *Guardian* newspaper ran its own investigations into the subject – and it too found that people in certain professions had planetary aspects in common.

Gauquelin's book, *The Cosmic Clocks*, has helped to give astrology a new credibility, and many Freudian- and Jungian-trained psychologists and analysts are now learning about astrology and using it in their work. The great majority of young people in Britain and America believe that there is something in it.

Astrology is not directly concerned with reincarnation, but has a very significant bearing on the subject. By far the great majority of astrologers take it as fact that reincarnation exists and that previous lives have a profound bearing on the present physical existence. Those who believe in cosmic forces – that we are interacting with the universe, with non-material energies and so on – almost always accept the idea of reincarnation. They find it easy to accept the idea that somehow, somewhere, everything balances up, that there is cosmic justice and a plan and order to everything we do. Serious astrologers cannot accept the old explanation of the scientists that everything is random, chance and essentially meaningless.

## Findhorn and the Wrekin Trust

A thriving community of several hundred people situated in the north of Scotland, Findhorn, very much a New Age institution, was founded in the early 1960s by Eileen and Peter Caddy and Dorothy Maclean. Their story began as a sad one. Peter had taken a job as a hotel manager but was made redundant. Both of the Caddys had led adventurous lives until then, and hoped that at last they would be able to settle in one place for a while. Unable to find a job, Peter Caddy went with his family to live in a caravan in a car park near an abandoned RAF base in Findhorn in 1962. They wondered what to do next, as they had no money and few prospects.

One day, Eileen heard an 'inner voice' speaking to her, saying: 'Know that I am God.' The voice went on to say that all her troubles were now over, if she would only be guided by what she heard. Eileen listened, as did her husband. Soon, the two of them were joined by their friend, Dorothy Maclean, and by others who said they had been brought by 'inner guidance' to form the spiritual community of Findhorn.

At the time, Findhorn was a barren place where nothing would grow. But the Caddys and others listened to their inner voices, which purported to be plant 'devas' or gods, and who would make things grow where nothing had before. The various channels were told that if they co-operated with each other and communicated with nature, they would see wonders appear. Sure enough, before long a beautiful garden began to flourish, with huge vegetables such as four-feet cabbages and flowers that would not normally grow in that part of the world. At least, that was the story. Again, it is easy to be sceptical. A book called *The Magic of Findhorn*, telling the story of how the community was started and flourished, contains no pictures of the amazing fruits and vegetables and the author, Paul Hawken, who visited the community in the early 1970s says he did not see any unusual-sized specimens. People who visit the place now say that the plants are of ordinary size.

Be that as it may, twenty-five years later Findhorn itself thrives and flourishes, and has been the subject of a number of television documentaries. It now has several hundred members living full-time in the community, a publishing company, a school and many other industries and enterprises. Those who have visited it say that they are aware of a tremendous and unusual feeling of co-operation, and most people experience a sense of spirituality and uplift when they go there. The 'believers' maintain that none of this would have happened without the work of cosmic forces, and the willingness of the Caddys to listen to what these forces were saying.

The Findhorn community do not have any corporate views on reincarnation, but Peter Caddy, who studied Rosicrucianism as a young man and travelled round India listening to doctrines about rebirth, accepts the concept. Certainly the community believe that, unless we accept the reality of the non-physical element in humans, we shall never make progress. It is this element which enables us to harmonize with the rest of nature.

The Wrekin Trust, which in many ways is the apotheosis of the New Age movement, does not owe its origin to any spirit from the starry spheres. It was founded in 1971 by Sir George Trevelyan, a former adult education lecturer who felt the time was right for an organization which could provide a forum for discussion and the bringing together of new scientific discoveries and age-old wisdom, in a modern spiritual context. Every year since its inauguration the Trust has held an annual 'Scientists and Mystics' residential conference, at which the speakers come from the worlds both of science and of mysticism. In addition, throughout the year the Trust holds hundreds of non-residential seminars and meetings which discuss such subjects as astrology, earth mysteries, the Kabbalah, new maths, new physics, new biology, parapsychology and the gaining of inner wisdom. The Trust has held a number of conferences on reincarnation, at which it has assembled speakers and experts on the subject from all over the world. It has probably done more than any other British organization to bring the subject of reincarnation back to respectability and give it a public airing. Usually there are speakers both for and against the belief, and all the latest research on the subject is discussed and evaluated. After the conference, tapes of all the important speeches are made available.

## The New Humanity Journal

This British publication was founded in 1975 as the world's first 'politico-spiritual' journal, and it openly accepts the idea of reincarnation. The idea is to merge the 'inner and the outer', and the journal looks forward to the day when there will be 'pneumatocracy' – which has nothing to do with Michelin men or car tyres, but means 'the rule of the spirit'.

The present editor of the journal, Johan Quanjer, a fifty-year-old Dutch former agriculturalist, feels that the age of the spirit is just round the corner. He also believes that nowadays reincarnation is coming out very much into the open, and has to be taken seriously by anybody who is working for a better world, who would like peace and harmony instead of strife and discord. His view is that a belief in reincarnation can help in many ways – even if you only pretend to believe it:

'At the very least, if you open your mind to the possibility of reincarnation, you become part of history, part of what has gone before and what is to come in the future. You start to believe that your actions may have consequences, and there is justice in the world, even if you can't always see it. A belief in reincarnation makes people much less harsh when judging their fellows, and it also paves the way for better relationships generally. These days, most of us view a family as a thirty-eight-year-old man, a thirty-six-year-old woman and two children ages ten and eight. But if you accept reincarnation, you have a far wider view of a family. Your children aren't yours, they are not your possessions, but simply souls in small bodies that you are looking after for the time being.

'In another incarnation, these children may have been your parents,

your neighbours, your lovers. You don't know. An understanding of reincarnation also helps with such guilt-laden subjects as abortion and
euthanasia. You cannot kill the body, only the soul. If the mother aborts a
child before it has a viable independent existence, that soul will just go and
find another body. Also, if you help a dying person on their way, you are
just releasing the soul from the body, helping it to shed a physical form that
no longer works.'

But couldn't a belief in reincarnation be used to justify murder? After
all, if we are just helping the soul to be released from the body . . . .

'Not at all, because if you believe in reincarnation, you automatically
take on board the concept that all actions will have to be accounted for, good
and bad. It's not that God punishes and rewards people, but that we create
our own circumstances for the future.'

Quanjer believes that people in general are far more open to the idea of
reincarnation than ever before, at least in modern times. 'I've seen a
phenomenal change just within the fourteen years that this journal has been
going', he said. 'When we started, we were very much considered part of
the arcane tradition, and were part of a minority movement the general
public knew very little about.

'Most people who were at all interested in the subject had heard of
Annie Besant, Madame Blavatsky and Rudolf Steiner, all of whom believed
implicitly in reincarnation. But actually between about 1875 and 1975 there
were literally hundreds of little orders of people who were into reincarnation, but who kept themselves behind drawn curtains. People belonging
to these little orders and groups were usually rather refined, very well-read
people who had worked out just how reincarnation happened, to their own
satisfaction, and who kept their knowledge to themselves.

'This wasn't because they wanted to keep it secret', Quanjer added.
'They would have loved to tell the world about themselves, but not enough
people were interested. So rather than risk being written off as complete
nutters, they just kept quiet. There were a very limited number of listeners.
In the twenties and thirties less than five per cent of the population were
what we should now call "inner-directed". Now, according to the latest
estimates, it's 37 per cent of the population.

'Things have changed radically. Even in 1957, only 15 per cent of
people in the UK were at all interested in these subjects. One of the reasons
for the greater openness about reincarnation is that people are far less rigid
than they used to be, and far less compartmentalized. The media explosion,
and new, instant, global communication techniques have opened up the

subject in a way that was just not possible before. Also, although the little tight enclosed orders of the past had very firm views on reincarnation, they all disagreed with each other. Some said that souls reincarnated after three hundred years, others that it happened almost at once, and nobody could prove one way or the other who was right, or wrong.'

From the first, the *New Humanity Journal* wanted to put the idea of reincarnation on a scientific footing, to see whether there was objective and logical evidence for the belief. Said Quanjer: 'We published some extremely scientific articles from physicists on how reincarnation might work mathematically, and this again helped to open the subject up. For the first time, trained scientists were taking the idea seriously. The trouble with a lot of early New Age people is that they tended to waffle and never be specific. But once properly trained scientists began investigating reincarnation, it gained a new respectability. We have published serious articles from physicists asking: what is it that reincarnates? What is conveyed to the next life?

'What has happened is that now, the ordinary person in the street is talking about reincarnation. It is no longer a hidden subject. It is even being used as a chat-up line now. Young men go up to women and say: ''I feel instantly attracted to you. We must have known each other in a previous incarnation. Can we continue the relationship?'' This is a misuse of the subject, of course, but also an indication of how far the thinking has now penetrated everyday occurrences.

'In the health field,' Quanjer said, 'the idea of reincarnation definitely helps. Roberto Assagioli, an Italian Jungian psychiatrist, has said that whenever people are open to the idea of a higher self, the spiritual, to reincarnation, they stand a 90 per cent chance of a cure. Otherwise, if they remain closed, their chances go down to 30 per cent. He said this from a strictly medical point of view, based on his findings over the years.' Both physical and psychiatric complaints can be helped in this way, since all illness can have a psychosomatic content.

Quanjer also believes that to be open to the possibility of reincarnation could help us to understand, and possibly overcome, the great problem of violence, particularly male violence, which has every Western nation worried. 'Some people say it's due to the influence of television, others that we have always lived in violent societies and that violence is part of being human. But one example may shed light on the problem of violence. One young man grew up to be a violent rebel. Nobody knew what to do with him and every time he struck out he used to say, ''I don't know what came over me.'' One day, however, he had some kind of mystical experience that he was a soldier in the Second World War, and while he was killing and fighting he died. As he spoke, his mother wrote down the name of the soldier and his details, then went to Washington to check them out. It was all as the young man had said in his "dream". He now realized just why he had been a hooligan, and understood that he was still fighting a battle, but he had no need to. This mystical experience cured him. So we can ask: who makes hooligans? Who sends young men to the battlefield? We don't have to blame TV – it's easy to see how society has produced hooligans.

'After fourteen years of editing this journal, and handling many articles on reincarnation, I have to say I don't understand it', Quanjer said. 'I receive all kinds of material, and can only say that there is no one simple explanation. We can only look at the therapeutic effects and ask ourselves whether such a belief benefits, or harms, humanity. To me, it explains so much that is otherwise unexplainable.

'What I do know is that the public is now thirsting for knowledge on this and related subjects. There is enormous interest now in whether we get messages from other planets. To me, it doesn't much matter whether we do or not. The important aspect is that a process is set in whereby we become familiar with the notion of being linked up to the cosmos. This whole movement has encouraged people to look farther outwards and also more deeply inward. The two go together.

'Reincarnation gives a meaning, a purpose to life that would be hard to find with any other explanation of why we are here. Of course, there is a lot of hocus pocus and there are probably a large number of charlatans about. The important thing in all this, though, is that our basic assumptions are now being called into question, and this means that things are moving. Our beliefs are no longer stagnant, as they were at the end of the 1950s.'

## Alternative medicine

Complementary or alternative medicine, once dismissed as 'fringe' or 'quackery', is now very much part of the mainstream. All such therapies have in common the idea that, rather than just look at the symptoms, they must take into account the whole person – mind, body and spirit. The 'holistic' movement, which was once considered very minority and New Age oriented, is now being taken seriously by an increasing number of orthodox doctors, medical schools and hospitals.

Holistic doctors are medically qualified, but they may use meditation, hypnosis, diet, relaxation, biofeedback, acupuncture, homeopathy or any other complementary therapy alongside their orthodox treatments.

The big breakthrough came when Lieutenant Colonel Marcus Macausland started a group called Health for the New Age. After retiring from the army, he suffered from a stroke which left him paralysed down one side. Ordinary doctors could not help him and in desperation he turned to Silva Mind Control, a method of positive thinking which had been developed by a Spanish American electronics engineer called José Silva. Through the power of positive thinking Macausland made a complete recovery, and began to realize that the mind, and mental attitudes, plays a very large part indeed in health and illness. Health for the New Age soon attracted a number of terminally ill cancer patients who had been told by their doctors that they were beyond hope. Macausland instituted a 'healing circle' in his home, to which practising psychics and paranormal healers would come to see if they could help the cancer patients. The patients were encouraged to carry on with their orthodox treatment at the same time as receiving paranormal help, and many made miraculous recoveries. It was also found that so-called spiritual therapies could often help cancer patients when nothing else could. Health for the New Age subsequently changed its name to Association for New Approaches to Cancer.

At the same time that Macausland was spreading the news about positive thought and the laying on of hands, Canon Christopher Pilkington and his wife, a radio broadcaster, founded the Bristol Cancer Help Centre, which also used meditation and spiritual therapies alongside diet and more conventional treatments. This Centre gained the royal seal of approval when Prince Charles officially opened it.

Then, in the early 1980s, the British Holistic Medical Association was founded for doctors, nurses and other medically qualified people, with the aim of ushering in a completely new approach to medicine and healing. Again, Prince Charles gave the BHMA his blessing when he paid a visit to the Lisson Grove Health Centre where the founder, Dr Patrick Pietroni, worked.

While these developments were taking place in the United Kingdom, similar revolutions were under way in America and Europe, Australia and South Africa. Nothing now was suspect any more – if it worked. The proof of the pudding had to be in the eating.

# Hypnosis and past-life regression

One of the strangest-sounding of all therapies, hypnotic regression – in which patients are regressed back into past lives – was having amazing successes with many psychosomatic disorders that would not respond to any form of conventional treatment. Now an ever-growing number of practitioners, who include medically qualified doctors and psychiatrists as well as hypnotherapists and those formerly considered 'unqualified', are using past-life therapy to treat emotional and phobic problems.

Past-life therapists work on the assumption that reincarnation is a fact. The patients do not have to believe this for the therapy to work; they do, however, have to be broadly sympathetic to the idea, otherwise they may strongly resist hypnosis or searching questions about themselves.

In their book *The Alternative Health Guide*, Brian Inglis and Ruth West write:

> If we have souls which survive death, or if reincarnation exists, it
> would not be surprising if traces of our past lives should
> periodically filter down into a present life, causing mental or
> emotional disturbance. Past lives therapy is based on the
> assumption that some disorders arise because of past lives
> burrowing their way, as it were, into an individual's
> subconscious, and that these psychic intrusions may need to be
> brought to the surface, on the same principle that Freud
> introduced psychoanalysis to bring up repressed traumas.

The practice of past-life therapy, at least in present times, began in America with the work of Los Angeles psychologist Morris Netherton, founder of the Institute for Past Lives Awareness. In his book, *Past Lives Therapy*, Netherton admits that his belief of past lives affecting the present will make many people extremely incredulous. Many of his own patients have expressed profound scepticism, saying that reincarnation has yet to be conclusively proved. Netherton says that he doubts whether reincarnation will *ever* be definitively proved one way or the other, but for the time being, to work on the assumption that it does exist is extremely helpful therapeutically. So far as Netherton is concerned, reincarnation works as a convenient hypothesis. What matters is whether it works – and it does, he says in his book.

One British psychiatrist who has had great success with past-life therapy is Dr Denys Kelsey. For very many years he worked in the psychiatric department of St Bartholomew's Hospital in London. Then he met Joan Grant, who was convinced she had lived many times before; Kelsey came to believe that Joan was absolutely genuine, and co-authored her most famous book, *Many Lifetimes*. Since the book was published in 1967 Dr Kelsey has been working in private practice, and is now absolutely convinced that past-life therapy is often the only way to help patients who are troubled by fears which seem to have no root cause.

Dr Kelsey uses hypnosis to enable patients to regress themselves into previous lives; other therapists use the talking method, which consists of a conversational approach to get patients back into other memories. Dr Kelsey said: 'I've now come to believe that very many traumas and phobias which people have are the results of experiences in previous lives. They are blocking energy for the present life.'

According to Kelsey, there are a number of indications that a previous life may hold the key to a present problem. 'In some way,' he said, 'the feelings are simply not appropriate to the present situation. The patient has no idea why there should be such a strong phobia, or what may have sparked it off.'

One young woman patient who came to see Dr Kelsey suffered from an absolute horror of flying. Her fear started when she went on her very first flight, and got worse and worse. It had not been activated by any accident or fright when on a plane. She went for therapy because her job involved flying, and yet she was terrified to do it.

Dr Kelsey put her under hypnosis, told her to count to ten, and then asked her to say what was in her mind. (All reputable hypnotists have to be careful not to put any suggestions into the patient's mind, as these will just be repeated when under hypnosis.) In this case, the patient started to explain that she had been a young man in the Second World War, on a mission which involved flying and jumping out of an aeroplane with a parachute. There was at this time no fear whatever of flying.

While still under hypnosis, the patient suddenly had great difficulty in speaking and said that her throat was full of blood. Her anxiety soon turned to horror as she realized the plane was on fire. She – then he – died before the plane hit the ground. She was then brought back to consciousness, and Dr Kelsey told her what she had said: the patient was astonished, as she had no memory of this at all – in fact, people rarely remember what they say under hypnosis when they are brought round. This patient had no idea she was harbouring these memories, but at once the phobia was cured.

Dr Kelsey said: 'Some people might try to explain this away by saying that my patient had, years before, seen a film such as *The Dam Busters* and then forgotten all about it, burying the memory. But that doesn't explain why thousands of other people have seen this film without developing the slightest fear of flying. Others might say that my patient concocted the story knowing that I believed in reincarnation, and used it in therapy. But if this was the case, why should her phobia have been cured?'

Dr Kelsey has believed in reincarnation for over twenty years, and says that for all that time this belief has been the cornerstone of his work as a psychiatrist. His feeling is that human beings must have within themselves a soul, or non-physical component as he prefers to call it, which lives on after the body has died. It is this non-physical element which reincarnates and which can be responsible for traumas, fears and emotional problems in the present.

'Freud showed convincingly that many adult problems have their roots in traumatic childhood events, and that these memories have often been suppressed. You can certainly encourage adults to relive traumatic childhood events under hypnosis. You can also regress them back to their babyhood and birth.'

A similar kind of treatment to past-life therapy is rebirthing, where people are taken back to their actual birth experience and, often, their foetal life. Dr Kelsey believes that when an egg and a sperm come together it is the energy provided by the incoming soul which enables the cell division to take place.

'To me,' he said, 'a belief in reincarnation sheds valuable light on a person's character. Why is it that in so many families, children are completely different from one another? Why do some children appear to have inborn gifts, such as for music and painting, when they could not possibly have been taught these in such a short lifetime? Why are some children irritable and bad-tempered while others born of the same parents are sunny and good-natured?

'These things can't just be explained away by social or hereditary factors. Most psychiatrists accept that there is a predisposition towards certain types of behaviour, but why should there be this predisposition? Where does it come from in the first place? I believe that a person's character is formed in the course of a very long history.

'Until we can recognize reincarnation as a reality, as I see it, we shan't have very much success in treating people with serious psychiatric disorders. It's only when we can unblock the energy connected with a past event that they can get well.'

Ray Keedey-Lilley, who had no formal medical training but found he had a natural talent as a healer, set up in practice as a hypnotist in the 1940s. In those days hypnosis was very much frowned on by orthodox medical practitioners, who considered it extremely suspect. Now, Keedey-Lilley spends most of his time training doctors and dentists and other members of the medical profession to use hypnosis in their treatment of problems. He has also used past-life therapy for very many years.

He said: 'I don't begin to understand how reincarnation works, or what all the ins and outs might be. All I know is that past-life therapy is extremely effective. It has a very high success rate.

'It all began for me,' he went on, 'when, under hypnosis, something occurred which couldn't be explained in ordinary terms. I had one man who came to me with a very bad stutter. During the second or third session of hypnosis he suddenly became very agitated and I asked him to tell me about it. He then started saying that he was standing in a large room lined with books and he was watching a man leading two hunters up to the house. My patient said that this man (the one in the room) was clearly him, and yet it wasn't. This all came out of the blue, and neither of us was prepared for it. The peculiar thing was that this past-life experience didn't have any bearing on his present problem as a stutterer.

'Another patient who came to me for lack of self-confidence seemed to remember a past life where she was watching a man die in the trenches in the First World War. Now, where did that memory come from?

'I do think that one has to be careful about past lives', Keedey-Lilley said. 'People can certainly manufacture past lives and there is no way of checking them out. I've also created past lives for people where I've mentioned something to them and they have told me about a past-life experience to explain their present problem. There is no doubt that if you are a devout believer in reincarnation you will put this interpretation on to fit your particular case. One of the main problems is that so little can be proved, and it is all so easy to criticize.

'But there is also no doubt that past-life therapy works. If you use it to explain a fear, the fear does usually go and the client loses the problem. One patient of mine was a young builder who had a horror of high places. Every time he went up on a piece of scaffolding, he would become terrified and say that they were coming for him. Of course, there was nobody there. Eventually he came for therapy as his fear was stopping him doing his job and he had to take a lot of time off ''sick''.

'I took him back to a past life and he remembered having been hanged.

Once that memory came to the surface, it could be erased, and trouble this patient no more. This man was a devout Catholic and didn't believe in reincarnation at all, yet it still worked for him.'

He went on to talk of another patient. 'A lady came to see me once, not because she had any problems, but because something completely inexplicable had occurred while she was on holiday in France with her husband. They were driving round Paris and suddenly she said, "I'll direct you." Since neither of them had been to Paris before, her husband felt she couldn't possibly know the way, but she insisted so much that he had to take notice of her.' And she did find the way.

## Spiritual healing

Most, if not all, spiritual healers base their entire work on the assumption that reincarnation is an indisputable fact. Spiritual healers are men and women, often without any formal medical qualifications, who work by channelling energy 'from a higher source' and then passing it on to the patient. If the patient is receptive to the energy, healing will take place.

Although healing is a very ancient art, as old as humanity itself, thirty years ago hardly anybody in the West had even heard of it. The combination of Christianity, which frowned on anything supernatural and psychic, and modern scientific medicine were enough to make healing fall into serious disrepute.

Then, in 1955, two years after the repeal of the Witchcraft Act – witches have practised healing since ancient times – the Confederation of Spiritual Healers was formed in Great Britain. Gradually, throughout the New Age, healing became increasingly more respectable and eventually was put to stringent scientific examination in Britain and America. Laboratory tests using sophisticated machines showed that, contrary to expectation, something really did happen when healing took place. People's brainwaves were altered, as measured on an electroencephalogram machine. In addition, there was very often a noticeable improvement in their actual illness.

Nowadays, of course, this kind of healing has become respectable. In the UK it is available under the National Health Service if recommended or carried out by a doctor. Several university departments are now conducting experiments to try and ascertain exactly what happens when a healer gets to

work. The British Royal College of Veterinary Surgeons is presently conducting an experiment with horses to see what effect, if any, spiritual
healing has on animal disorders.

Healers work in a completely different way from ordinary doctors.
They have to understand that they are acting simply as instruments, as
channels for this 'higher energy', and they have to take complete responsibility for the work they do. The point of healing is not necessarily to effect
a cure, although this does often happen, but to enable the patient to get in
touch with his or her inner self and to create a situation where healing is
possible. Philippa Pullar, author of several books on spiritual healing, has
written: 'A spiritual healer is creating a possibility for the patient to become
linked with the origin and essence of the spiritual force.' In this context, the
word 'spiritual' refers to the divine source of energy. It has nothing to do
with spiritualism, with getting in touch with discarnate entities or spirits;
neither has it anything to do with any organized religion.

Nor is spiritual healing, explains Philippa Pullar, the same as faith
healing. The patient does not have to have 'faith' in order for the healing to
work; he or she just needs to be receptive to the idea. Even if the patient is
not receptive, or does not even know about the healing, it can still take
place. This is why experiments are now being undertaken with animals. If
it can be shown objectively that animals improve when given healing, this
will indicate that the effect is not merely placebo, or all in the mind. Absent
and animal healing are part of the work undertaken by most spiritual
healers. From her home in London one animal healer, Sylvia Crystal
Broadwood, has had great success in healing animals as far away as
Australia and America, and her work has been endorsed by several
orthodox vets.

Healers believe that we do not just possess the physical body but that
essentially we are spirits temporarily housed in a physical overcoat. We
become ill, not so much because our bodies might be invaded by alien
germs, bacteria or viruses, but because our physical, mental and spiritual
energies have become blocked by negativity. This negativity can be
accumulated over several lifetimes and goes some way to explaining why
children may be born handicapped, prematurely, or develop cancer in their
early years. We are not born with a clean slate, but with the accumulated
remnants, for good or bad, of very many lifetimes. Philippa Pullar writes:
'The physical form of Man is but a temporary dwelling house for the spirit
as it gains further experience in the world of matter.'

The healing energy, she explains, is exactly the same energy which is used for making money, to produce works of art or establish a successful career. The very highest form of this vital force is manifest in geniuses. In the same way, healers vary. Although healing is considered to be a gift, there are both geniuses and those with very limited talent in the field of healing.

Centuries ago most illness, whether mental or physical, was understood to be the work of demons or evil spirits. Gradually this idea came to be discredited as primitive superstitious nonsense. But spiritual healers do accept that evil, or ill-intentioned spirits, might lie in wait to inhabit or possess the weak and defenceless. In ancient times all healing was exorcism – casting out evil spirits. Now, say spiritual healers, this knowledge of harmful spirits is being resurrected. The idea is that if a person becomes strong and harmonious within, there will be no room for an evil spirit to enter.

The state of mind of the healer is also important in enabling curative powers to be released. When we go to an ordinary doctor we expect him or her to be able to cure us, whatever their own state of mind or health. Doctors are allowed to drink, smoke, be promiscuous and watch pornographic movies, if they so wish, without any idea that their healing powers might be affected. Spiritual healers, by contrast, have to be very careful to keep themselves pure and clean, so that the healing energy can flow through them. This energy, they believe, can be blocked by drinking, smoking, taking mind-altering drugs or over-indulging in sex. The patient, too, must become pure and clean in order to be well. Again, this idea is hardly current in modern orthodox medicine. We expect that we can be made better without putting any effort in ourselves, without giving up drinking, altering our diets, or trying to make sure we are not consumed by negative thoughts.

Essentially, spiritual healing is holistic medicine. It heals the mind, body and spirit all at once and makes no distinction between the three. These days, spiritual healers work very much in conjunction with conventional doctors, and always ask their patients to continue with their orthodox treatment as well as proceeding with the spiritual healing. Spiritual healers do not claim to be able to mend broken bones or perform essential surgery, or to be an effective substitute for these. All they do is to release a potent form of energy, rather like electricity, which can set the healing process in motion.

Spiritual healers do not always claim to be able to cure. In fact, sometimes they see their work as helping people to die peacefully. Philippa Pullar says: 'We have made such giants out of illness and death. We have to realise that death is not the end but a transition.' Healing, she says, is not just a matter of helping people to live longer, but also enabling them to 'cross over', to take the fear and terror out of death and dying. She adds:

> It can take many lives to work out our difficulties so that we can find this essential unity. Life after life we reach for ourselves until finally we can see our whole journey from beginning to end. We realise that completeness of ourselves, the integration of every life and the wisdom beyond. Our mission on earth will have been accomplished.

Not long ago, such sentiments would have been kept quiet or, if published, confined to journals and books not intended for the general market. It is a sign of the times that a major paperback publisher, Penguin, commissioned Philippa Pullar to write a book on spiritual healing, and asked her to include the concepts of etheric bodies, auras, healing energies, channels and reincarnation as a matter of course.

These ideas no longer seem so strange, and there is little doubt that healing does work. There are now four thousand members of the National Federation of Spiritual Healers in Britain, and more people are learning how to heal all the time. According to practitioners, genuine healing, which is always self-healing, cannot take place unless and until the patient accepts the spiritual dimension of illness, and can take on board the idea that he or she is basically a spirit, temporarily housed in a body. The spirit will live for ever and ever and be constantly reincarnated, but the successive bodies will wither and die.

## Multiple personality and possession

Recently, as radical psychologists and psychiatrists have returned to the idea that some patients suffering from certain mental disorders might be possessed by disembodied spirits, they have used this theory to try and shed light on multiple personality disorder. In this most intriguing and baffling of all mental problems, the sufferer seems to exhibit many different types of personality, each of which bears no obvious relationship to the main one.

In fiction the most famous example of multiple, or at least split, personality is Robert Louis Stevenson's story of Dr Jekyll and Mr Hyde, in which good Dr Jekyll changed into evil Mr Hyde when he took a certain drug; in this account, the man underwent physical conversion as well. The 'multiple personality' idea is also contained in lycanthropy stories, in which an apparently ordinary and harmless young man changes into a werewolf every full moon. Fairy stories such as Beauty and the Beast contain an element of the multiple personality as well, when the handsome young man is revealed when the lady dares to kiss the beast. And today, horror films often take as their theme the idea that a man or woman can be 'possessed' or taken over, and then act in strange or uncharacteristic ways.

There have also been several real-life examples of multiple personality, the most famous being a successful film called *The Three Faces of Eve*. Books on real-life multiples include *The Minds of Billy Mulligan, Sybil* and *When Rabbit Howls*, a study of a woman who apparently had as many as ninety-two separate personalities existing within the one body.

The standard psychiatric explanation is that these apparently quite separate personalities are simply different aspects of the same psyche exhibiting themselves at times of stress or anxiety. It has been noticed that most people who suffer from multiple personality disorder, or MPD, have a history of trauma and problems, often starting in early childhood. This would bear out what has been discovered by the spiritual healers, who say that when we are negative or weak we are open to the influences of evil spirits roaming round the earth, who lie in wait for suitable people to enter.

Orthodox psychiatry of course discounts any such explanation. Most modern psychiatrists would say that all human beings can exhibit apparently quite different personalities on occasion, and that these come out as a defence against trauma, or perhaps to conform to cultural pressures. For instance, a man might be expected to appear strong, dominant and in command at work, while a woman might feel constrained to appear a loving, caring wife and mother – yet these culturally imposed 'personalities' may actually be quite distinct from the 'real' one underneath. The 'real' one, which may come as a shock and surprise to others, will only manifest itself under extreme pressure.

But the idea of possible possession by an alien spirit has never entirely gone away. As long ago as 1909 William James wrote 'that the demon-theory . . . will have its innings again is to my mind absolutely certain. One has to be ''scientific'' indeed to be blind and ignorant enough to suspect no such possibility.'

American psychiatrist Ralph B Allison has studied multiple personality patients extensively, and has come to the conclusion that there is at least a possibility of spirit possession. He says that there is a whole spectrum of disorders here, ranging from part of the person's own mind apparently splitting off to a situation in which the entire human being seems to have been taken over by a completely alien personality. Allison has stated that there often appears to be 'possession by demonic spirits from satanic realms, and that's an area I don't care to discuss or be part of'. He admits, though, that it is at least 'a theoretical possibility'.

Certainly conventional psychiatry has no adequate explanation for multiple personality disorder, or any method of curing the problem apart from giving drugs to reduce the effects of the different personalities. But when the effects of the drugs wear off, the alien personalities are liable to come out again.

For those who accept reincarnation, there are two possible explanations of MPD. One is that the human being is indeed invaded or taken over by a demonic spirit which wishes to control and command, and who, although discarnate, wishes to be part of a physical body again. Spiritual healers would say that such spirits have never really been able to accept that they are no longer housed in a physical body, and that in the meantime they are inhabiting somebody else's. Many years ago the medium Dion Fortune wrote a book called *Psychic Self-Defence* which described how to protect oneself from invading spirits.

Another possible explanation of the disorder is that bits and pieces of previous personalities, lifetimes or experiences keep breaking through present consciousness. They have not merged in the present incarnation.

The idea of possession is quite different from channelling, mentioned earlier, as the channels operate as vehicles for spirits or entities who are essentially benevolent and wish to help humans on the earthly plane. When a person is 'possessed', however, he or she is being taken over by a malevolent entity, who only wishes to do harm and damage.

All nonsense? Well, to those schooled in rational modern thinking it certainly sounds so. But we must bear in mind that nobody, however clever, has yet been able to offer an adequate explanation for MPD. It is, in its most extreme manifestations, a fairly rare disorder, but one which still has psychiatry completely baffled.

## Shirley MacLaine

Undoubtedly the person who has had most influence on current ideas about reincarnation is the film star Shirley MacLaine. Her several books on the subject – all personal – have become world bestsellers and Shirley is now in great demand as a speaker at seminars all over America.

Shirley MacLaine has become the modern guru on the subject of the mind, body and spirit, and in some ways there could hardly be a better one. She is rich, successful, beautiful, world-famous and has a string of household-name films such as *Irma La Douce* behind her. Shirley is also the sister of one of the Western world's most enduring sex symbols, Warren Beatty; and she is also something of a sex symbol herself, although now well into her fifties.

There is an enormous amount of interest today in what Shirley Maclaine is saying. Her books have been eagerly read and digested by hundreds of thousands of people who never before even considered the possibility of reincarnation.

Her first book on reincarnation, *Out on a Limb*, begins as a personal quest for identity. On page 48 her friend David – the two significant men in this book, 'David' and 'Gerry', the latter supposedly a British politician, have never been identified, although numerous guesses have been made – asks Shirley whether she believes in reincarnation. Shirley, at this time 'resting' at her beach house in Malibu, is astonished at the question. David then goes on to say that when you have studied the occult as long as he has, it's not a question of whether or not it's true, but of how it works.

Intrigued, Shirley began to read all she could about the occult and arcane traditions, and rapidly became extremely knowledgeable. She discovered that many ancient and modern philosophers and thinkers have quite seriously held the view that the soul is immortal and embodies itself time and time again, until it is purified and needs to be embodied no more. At the same time as Shirley was discovering all this, she was conducting a global relationship with Gerry who, needless to say, remained completely unconvinced by all this. The function of Gerry in this book, apart from the obligatory sex interest, seems to be as a kind of Dr Watson to Sherlock Holmes – he asks all the questions that the ordinary 'man in the street' might ask. But unlike Dr Watson he does not become convinced and remains a typical sceptic, hardly willing to listen to the answer, and wondering whether Shirley is quite mad.

Notwithstanding the sceptical Gerry, Shirley pursues her quest and ends up in Peru with David, who tells her of his experiences with Mayan, an extra-terrestrial from the Pleiades. It is at this point that the sympathetic reader starts to wonder. Reincarnation may be one thing, but communication with beautiful extra-terrestrials in Peru? It all sounds very much like science fiction but it is, however, presented as fact, and Shirley has since appeared on numerous television programmes to defend all the statements made in *Out on a Limb*.

The upshot of the book is that Shirley comes to believe in reincarnation as an absolute fact. She consults mediums and channels, and is told that she had a relationship in a previous life with both Gerry and David. With David it was good, but with Gerry it was problematic on both previous occasions. This time, however, it all works itself out to a satisfactory conclusion: Shirley tells us that the relationship with Gerry cools and dies.

Whether the stories and experiences related in *Out on a Limb* are true can never be proved, but a TV company found the book interesting enough to make a mini-series out of it. The mini-series enabled Shirley to write another book on the subject. And so it goes on. The experiences related in these books are easy to laugh at and easy enough to knock down. Arch-debunker Henry Gordon's *Channeling into the New Age* considers Shirley MacLaine at best a muddled and vague thinker. Science fiction writer Isaac Asimov, who wrote the introduction to Gordon's book, says that the New Age in general, and MacLaine in particular, is so much gibberish:

> There is the absolute refusal to accept the fact of death. We are the only species we know of, now or ever, that has discovered that this is inevitable for every individual. In reaction, the vast majority of us simply deny that death is death, and fervently believe in ghosts, in spirit worlds, in an afterlife, in the transmigration of souls. The evidence in favour of immortality of any part of ourselves is absolutely zero, but the will to believe easily overcomes that little matter . . . .

Here we have Henry Gordon writing a book that considers the MacLaine story to be nonsense and debunks it.

Will this harm MacLaine? I doubt it. Will it win away the helpless innocents who pant after her 'gibberish'? I doubt it.

Then why bother?

First, there's a matter of self-respect. If one is fortunate enough to be gifted with a modicum of rationality, he or she has the responsibility to use it, even if the matter seems hopeless.

Asimov and Gordon share an absolute conviction that anybody who even considers the possibility of reincarnation, of the spirit world, of extra-terrestrials, of discarnate entities or channels, is so gullible as to be beyond hope. The New Age, explains Gordon, encompasses the entire field of the paranormal, and 'all irrational beliefs associated with it'. For him, these irrational beliefs include yoga, mysticism, all forms of alternative medicine, reincarnation, biorhythms and the new physics. Gordon says that the biologist Lyall Watson, who has written books saying, for example, that cars can sometimes possess the power to drive off by themselves and kill people, is writing 'the crowning heights of claptrap'. The quartz crystal has, he goes on, become a kind of symbol of the age, imbued with all kinds of mystical and spiritual powers. Yet, he maintains, there is not the slightest evidence for all these beliefs, and those who embrace them are being conned on a giant scale.

Gordon saves most of his vitriol for Shirley MacLaine because, he says, her books are presented as serious philosophical thoughts which are designed to influence the reader. Their message is masked by an easy, anecdotal style which can hold many traps for the unwary reader.

MacLaine, he thinks, is becoming to the spirit what Jane Fonda was to the body, and with about as much razmatazz and money-making involved. He wonders how so many people can possibly believe in her as a guru, as a fount of wisdom and knowledge, when so much of what she says is either patent nonsense or simply can't be corroborated. When MacLaine goes into detail about past lives no proof of any kind is given, he complains.

In answer to his own question about how people can seriously flock to MacLaine's seminars, he says that most of the attendees are women. That must explain it – women are so much less rational, so much more gullible, and have so much more time to waste, than men.

Whatever their viewpoint, both MacLaine's and Gordon's books get the reincarnation debate aired publicly. They have encouraged large numbers of people to start thinking about a subject which had most probably never entered their heads before. And as the readers start to think, they may wonder if perhaps it is not such arrant unprovable nonsense after all. Even Henry Gordon admits: 'Reincarnation is an appealing notion, and to some, a necessary source of hope and comfort. As a religious belief or a philosophical idea, it is difficult to dispute. I have no quarrel with a belief based on faith, but when Shirley MacLaine goes into great detail about past lives, hers and others, without proof of any kind, it becomes ludicrous.'

There is evidence that, nowadays, increasing numbers of people would like to believe in reincarnation. Increasingly large numbers of people are starting to think that it is the only explanation which seems to make some sense of life, of the universe, of why we are here. But one question that many sceptics ask is: if we all had past lives, why can so few of us remember anything about them? Why do so many of us go through our present life without the slightest indication that we have ever lived before? The next chapter looks at the experiences of those who have claimed past lives, and at the work of scientists and researchers who have attempted to provide conclusive objective proof for the existence of reincarnation.

# CHAPTER FOUR

# *People who have claimed previous lives*

Throughout this century, a considerable number of people have claimed that they have lived before. Sometimes their stories are vague and insubstantial, impossible to check out or ascertain in any way. But a few have been extremely vivid and detailed – so detailed that they are difficult to dismiss as mere fantasies or products of an overheated imagination. Most of the really famous stories have been subjected to intense investigation to see whether they really are examples of a previous life or whether there is some other, more ordinary explanation – such as that the subject has some time ago read a historical novel and has then consciously forgotten all about it. In certain cases, the 'historical novel' explanation provides a plausible answer, but some stories of claimed previous lives are not so easily dismissed.

## Joan Grant

The name of Joan Grant burst upon an astonished world in 1937, with the publication of her book *Winged Pharaoh*. The book reads like an exciting historical novel of Egypt in the First Dynasty, and contains all the ingredients essential for a compulsive read – mystery, intrigue, love, sex, violence, struggles, an authentic and exotic background, good triumphing over evil, bits and pieces of wisdom, poems, interesting and believable characters. The reading world was even more astonished when, two years later, Joan Grant published another historical novel, *Life as Carola*. This was the heartrending story of an illegitimate orphan who became a strolling player in sixteenth-century Italy.

Five more novels followed from Joan's prolific pen – stories set in biblical times, among the ancient Indians of America, and another in dynastic Egypt. The books became bestsellers and were marketed as historical novels, but the strangest thing about them was that they were all supposedly autobiographies of the author's colourful past. She did not research any of her books and said that she knew nothing of the times in which they were set – all she did was to 'shift level' and go into a kind of dream state in which she would dictate the stories, sometimes pouring out four or five thousand words at a time. As tape recorders had not been invented in those days, both her first and then second husbands, Leslie Grant and Charles Beatty, agreed to take down the novels from dictation.

Joan Marshall was born in 1907, the only child of Blanche and Jack Marshall. Her father was an extremely rich scientist, the world's foremost expert on mosquitoes. He was determined that his daughter should have a 'boy's' education, and decided that she should go to Cambridge and become a mathematician. Joan, however, rebelled, and instead got married at an early age to Leslie Grant, who was at the time studying to become a barrister. Later he became an archaeologist.

Ever since she could remember, Joan had experienced extremely vivid dreams which to her were more than dreams – they were occasions on which she met other people. As a child she was absolutely convinced that she had lived before, but it was not until she became an adult that she was able to 'shift level' and develop a technique that she called 'far memory' to enable her to go back into previous lifetimes.

Her parents knew many famous people and her father, a committed atheist who said that cathedrals made him feel sick, used to invite members of the Society for Psychical Research down to stay for the weekend. One of these was Sir Oliver Lodge, a founder of the SPR, who was in contact with his son who had been killed in the First World War. Joan said in her autobiography, *Far Memory*, that she soon came to realize that most mediums had only a small talent, and that mediumship was in fact a very rare gift. But in her family such things were not ruled out.

One weekend the teenage Joan met H.G. Wells, who was a house guest at her parents' home, and felt enough confidence to talk about her private dream world to him. Wells said to Joan: 'It's important that you become a writer.' She told him that her father had wanted her to become a mathematician, and that anyway she couldn't spell and was hopeless at writing. Nevertheless she read a lot and, although not highly educated, she was extremely literate.

Nothing much happened on the writing front as Joan entered into the kind of life that most upper-class young ladies led in those days – balls, young men, spending money, buying dresses, going to Paris and so on. Although many people already found her strange, several young men fell in love with her and she became engaged to someone whom she met in Paris. But during the time they were planning their marriage Joan became convinced that she never would marry Esmond, and was not surprised to hear that he had been killed in a shooting accident.

After this, the quality of her dreams changed and she would meet Esmond on another planet. During these dreams, Esmond would tell Joan that her body was not ready to die. Since childhood days, Joan had always felt quite separate from her body, as if it was a suit of clothes that she could take off and put on. When, later, she married Leslie Grant, she taught herself to wake up several times during the night and write down her dreams. Sometimes, during these dreams, she would be in another incarnation.

She confided to her husband her wish to become an author; but he was contemptuous, telling her that she never would be published. In fact, Leslie – according to Joan's accounts – appeared to be what today would be considered a typical young male chauvinist pig, wanting only an ordinary, stay-at-home wife and mother. Even so, he agreed to take down from dictation her dream sequences as they grew stronger, and as more characters appeared.

She accompanied Leslie on an archaeological expedition in 1934, spending twenty-five days in Egypt. When she came back to Scotland, where they were living, she decided to develop the faculty of 'far memory' and write down everything that streamed into her mind. Her idea at the time was to write down a story for a friend, Daisy, who had cancer; there was some urgency, because Daisy had only a short time to live. The result was *Winged Pharaoh*.

Although Leslie was happy to take down the stories from dictation, he was appalled at the prospect of any of his friends finding out about the 'far memory' experiences. He wanted it all kept a secret, and when Joan told him she was thinking of trying to get the stories published he made the immortal remark: 'Leslie Grant's wife thinks she was Pharaoh. What a thing to overhear in a club!'

Joan explained to Leslie that she was not Pharaoh, nor Carola, but simply shared part of her spirit with these previous people. She explained to him: 'The soul usually becomes part of the spirit after the body dies. Sometimes a part of the soul fails to integrate and the result is a ghost. When I am doing far memory all I do is to become aware of the spirit, which includes Sekeeta and Carola and all the others.' For there were more – both male and female, throughout many past ages and cultures. Joan explained to Leslie that Joan and Sekeeta, the Egyptian princess, were like two beads on the same necklace, and the memory they shared was contained in the string.

Leslie remained unconvinced and Joan thought no more about publication until, at a wedding in London, she met a friend, Guy McGraw, who asked her what she did with herself buried away in Scotland. Did she shoot grouse, and if so, however did she spend her time when the grouse were not in season?

Joan replied: 'I catch an occasional trout when I'm not too busy, but I spend most of my time remembering who I used to be when I lived in Egypt during the First Dynasty.'

'Good God, Joan! Have you gone off your head?' McGraw said, and then added, when he noticed she was laughing: 'You gave me quite a shock. I didn't realize you were joking'

'I'm not joking' Joan told him. 'I have dictated about sixty thousand words of what, even if you think I made it up, is an interesting story.'

The upshot of all this was that McGraw asked to see the manuscript, which Joan had brought to London with her for Daisy to read, and show it to a publisher, Arthur Barker. Barker was enthralled with the book and wanted to publish it immediately. Joan was worried, and told Daisy, 'If Arthur publishes it, the way I wrote the book is bound to get about, and then Leslie will be furious.'

Joan was certain that the book would be a total failure, and was worried when Barker decided to print two thousand copies. She had visions of hundreds of unsold copies mouldering away in the barn at her house in Scotland. But, like her later 'historical novels', it became an instant bestseller.

At first, Joan was content to have her books described and treated as historical novels. But in the collected paperback edition, published by Corgi in 1975, she stated quite categorically: 'During the past twenty years, seven books of mine have been published as historical novels which to me are biographies of previous lives I have known.' Her books are now out of print, sadly, and are not even obtainable in many libraries. The importance of that first novel in 1937 was that it opened people's eyes to the possibility that we may have lived before. After all, Joan Grant was not mad, she was not courting publicity, she came from a family of the utmost respectability and standing in society, she was a beautiful and cultured hostess – so they had to be taken seriously, at least up to a point.

The publication of *Winged Pharaoh* heralded the end of Joan's first marriage, and she subsequently married Charles Beatty. During the 1950s, that marriage too broke up, and she met the psychiatrist Denys Kelsey who was ten years younger.

Dr Kelsey became convinced that Joan Grant was genuine, and her experiences with previous lives led him to abandon his work as a conventional psychiatrist and concentrate on treating mental disorders by hypnotic regression. Joan and Denys married in 1967 and worked together as therapists and advisers; by this time both of them were absolutely convinced that we have all had very many previous lives, the traumas of which can often explain problems in the present. A submerged memory from a past life often bubbles up to interfere with the present – and has to be exorcised and explained before it can vanish.

## Bridey Murphy

In 1952 psychologist Morey Bernstein was hypnotizing American housewife Ruth Simmons when she started talking about a previous life as 'Bridey Murphy', an Irish woman who had lived centuries earlier. The book which was eventually published, called *The Search for Bridey Murphy*, sold well over a million copies and was the starting point for serious investigation of claimed past lives.

Ruth Simmons was a Colorado housewife who for fun agreed to put herself under hypnosis as an experiment. Under hypnosis she regressed to childhood, and starting talking about toys she had possessed when she was only one year old. Nobody considered there was anything strange about this, but in a subsequent session Bernstein told Simmons that this time she would be going further back. He said to his subject: 'Your mind will be going back . . . back until you find yourself in some other scene, in some other place, in some other time. You will be able to talk to me about it and answer my questions.'

Before long, still under hypnosis, Ruth Simmons began to relate the story of how she was an Irish girl called Bridey Murphy who lived in Cork with her mother Kathleen, her father Duncan, who was a barrister, and her brother. The year was 1806. More details soon rushed out.

At the age of fifteen she had attended Mrs Stryne's school in Cork, and later she married a man called Brian McCarthy, after which they went to live in Belfast. The hypnotism sessions continued, and ended with the death of Bridey at the age of sixty-six. After physical death, Bridey apparently lived in the spirit world for forty years and was then reborn in Iowa, in 1923, where she became the present Ruth Simmons.

After completing the tape recordings, Bernstein decided to check the facts with the Irish Consulate, the British Information Service and the New York Public Library. He discovered that many of Bridey's statements checked out with known historical facts, while Ruth Simmons had never visited Ireland in her life. So how could Ruth have known these things about Ireland, particularly in the last century – unless, of course, there was such a thing as reincarnation?

Many possibilities were explored to try and explain this phenomenon. So far as anybody knew, such an experiment had never been conducted before – at least, not with such dramatic results. Could Ruth have read about Bridey Murphy somewhere, and then consciously forgotten about her? Could somebody have told her these stories while she was a child, and then she had buried them deep in her memory? The possibility of crypto-mnesia – a condition in which facts that have been once learned become inaccessible to ordinary memory – was put forward. There was also the question of extra-sensory perception, or telepathy. If ESP existed – nobody was quite sure in those days – that might explain how this ordinary housewife had got hold of some unusual information.

Whatever the truth of the Bridey Murphy story – and it has never been finally resolved one way or the other – it unleashed a torrent of literature about reincarnation and the 'unexplained.' Many scientific papers on the subject poured forth from American universities, and well-known para-psychologists of the day put the story through their most stringent tests.

According to Henry Gordon, author of *Channelling into the New Age*, the story of Bridey Murphy began the whole current 'reincarnation craze': 'This case spawned a book, long-playing records, syndicated newspaper articles and magazine pieces, the sale of movie rights and worldwide attention. It kicked off a reincarnation craze which swept Western society.' But, Gordon continues, there was eventually an extremely simple explanation. Further investigation revealed that a Bridey Murphy lived across the street from Ruth Simmons when she was a little girl. This real Bridey used to tell stories about events in Ireland in the previous century. Consciously, the subject had forgotten all about these, but 'with the usual type of fantasizing', says Gordon, she projected herself back into that period. Henry Gordon thus dismisses the whole Bridey Murphy case, although he mentions that Dr Ian Stevenson, the foremost researcher into claimed previous lives today, remains impressed with the documentation of this case, and still feels it to be genuine.

Although the story of Bridey Murphy is important in that it focused attention on the whole question of reincarnation, in itself it is not particularly interesting, as it is the story of one rather dull and eventless life told by another person leading a dull and eventless life. Joan Grant's stories are very much more interesting and exciting, as they have exotic locations and at the same time as telling a fascinating story, dispense pieces of eternal wisdom. In *Life as Carola*, for instance, there are many conversations with wise people reflecting on the nature of love, on God and the universe, on the place of humans in the scheme of things, and on how eternal justice is worked out. It is these factors which give the books their appeal, and which set them apart from the ordinary historical novel.

## Arthur Guirdham and the Cathars

Here again is a story of reincarnation which cannot be easily dismissed as fraud or fakery and which involves people with impeccable professional reputations. In 1961 Dr Arthur Guirdham was a psychiatrist working in Bath when a patient, 'Mrs Smith', came to him complaining of persistent nightmares. She had been suffering these nightmares ever since she was a small child, and had always felt herself to be in some way different from other people.

Dr Guirdham discovered that Mrs Smith had been experiencing really dreadful dreams of murder and massacre for many years, and thought at first that she must be neurotic. He examined her, using the usual tests for neurosis, but discovered that her case did not fit these patterns. At the time, Mrs Smith was a housewife in her early thirties with two small children and a part-time job. Dr Guirdham stated in an interview: 'She was a perfectly sane, ordinary housewife. There was certainly nothing wrong with her mental faculties.'

She gave Dr Guirdham some stories and poems she had written as a schoolgirl. They were nightmarish stories about life in France as one of the Cathar sect in the thirteenth century, a branch of Roman Catholicism which believed in reincarnation and was eventually wiped out by the Inquisition. Mrs Smith had never been taught at school about the Cathars, and had never studied their history in any way. The case intrigued Dr Guirdham enough to send Mrs Smith's papers to a Professor Nelli of Toulouse University, who was an expert on Cathar history. He wrote back to say that in his opinion Mrs Smith's stories were an accurate description of life among the Cathars in that area in the Middle Ages.

Encouraged by having a sympathetic ear at last, Mrs Smith recounted further stories to Dr Guirdham, including a horrific account of how she had been burned at the stake. Guirdham reproduced this account in his book *The Cathars and Reincarnation*, published in 1970:

> The pain was maddening. You should pray to God when you're dying, if you can pray when you're in agony. In my dream I didn't pray to God . . . . I didn't know that when you were burnt to death you'd bleed. [The Inquisition's favourite form of killing was burning at the stake, as they were not allowed to shed blood, being a religious order.] But I was bleeding heavily. The blood was dripping and hissing in the flames. I wished I had enough blood to put the flames out. The worst part was my eyes. I hate the thought of going blind . . . .
>
> The flames weren't so cruel after all. They began to feel cold. Icy cold. It occurred to me that I wasn't burning to death but freezing to death. I was numb with the cold and suddenly I started to laugh. I had fooled those people who thought they could burn me. I am a witch. I had magicked the fire and turned it into ice.

Until this time Dr Guirdham had never believed in reincarnation, or even given the matter a minute's thought. But when Mrs Smith recounted further details of her previous Cathar life, even mentioning that Dr Guirdham himself had been one of them – her lover in that incarnation – he started to take it all more seriously.

In 1967 he visited the South of France with his wife and investigated Mrs Smith's claims for himself. He gained special permission to look at contemporary manuscripts and found to his surprise that Mrs Smith's dream recall had been completely accurate. She was able to give Dr

Guirdham names of places, events, people – all of which stood up to the most rigorous investigation. 'There was no way,' Dr Guirdham said, 'that she could have known about them. Even of the songs she wrote as a child, we found four in the archives. They were correct word for word.' Professor Nelli, probably the world's greatest authority on the period, confirmed everything, saying that what Mrs Smith had related was Cathar ritual down to the last detail. Dr Guirdham said: 'Professor Nelli is a most meticulous and sceptical assessor of evidence.'

As time went on, Dr Guirdham discovered more and more people in his locality who had apparently been Cathars in the thirteenth century, and who had all known each other in this previous lifetime. Mrs Smith began to dream in fluent French, and identified a number of friends and neighbours who were all together so many centuries ago. A synchronization of thought then started to happen between Dr Guirdham and Mrs Smith, who was definitely psychic and had powers of precognition. This, the first recorded case of 'group reincarnation', has baffled people interested in the subject since Guirdham wrote his books in the early 1970s.

What is the explanation? As many commentators on the case have said, if you don't believe it is a case of reincarnation, you have to find some other explanation which fits. But what could that possibly be? Exhaustive enquiries have established that 'Mrs Smith' could have had no way of knowing about the Cathar material which was so extraordinarily vivid in her dreams.

Although an alternative explanation has been found to convince sceptics about the Bridey Murphy case, no such non-reincarnation theory seems to fit the Guirdham story. For committed reincarnationists it is genuine proof; to others it remains a mystery. Some researchers have suggested that the whole thing might have been produced by a kind of group hysteria, or by people putting too much emphasis on their dreams.

The one drawback of the story is that Mrs Smith, who started the whole thing off, has remained anonymous and has never come forward to tell her version. It might be possible to accuse Dr Guirdham of making the whole thing up, except that one identified person, a Miss Clare Mills, also supposedly a member of the Cathar sect, came forward to confirm everything. Miss Mills was capable of automatic writing – she could spontaneously go into a trance and receive supposed messages from disembodied spirits, which she would then write down – and gave more information about the Cathar beliefs.

Apparently, she said, Cathars could withdraw into their spiritual bodies so that they would not be harmed by the flames when being burned at the stake. They were against procreation, as they believed this was only a way of imprisoning more spirits in flesh and prolonging the suffering that habitation in a physical body would inevitably cause. Those who managed to renounce sex and the things of this world, were known as *'parfaits'*. The group was unusual in those days in that both men and women could become *parfaits*, members of the elevated priesthood. On the anniversary of many members being burned at the stake, the Guirdham group all became affected by a strange illness.

But even for those who believe in recincarnation, many questions remain. Although the chain of coincidences and relationships seems too strange to admit of an ordinary explanation, why is it that this group of people should apparently have had only one incarnation in the past, and one which happened so very long ago? It is the belief of all reincarnationists that we have many lifetimes. An explanation of this could be, of course, that although this group had separately experienced many lifetimes since, it was only the Cathar one which imprinted itself deep in the memory, because of the intense trauma of the experiences.

# Omm Sety

From the age of three, in 1907, Dorothy Eady, who lived in a London flat with her parents, became convinced that England was not her real home. Instead, she kept saying, she belonged to Ancient Egypt. It all started when one day Dorothy fell down the stairs. A doctor was called for and pronounced the child dead. Dorothy's mother telephoned her husband, master tailor Reuben Eady, to come home at once, but when Reuben arrived home he found his little daughter sitting up in bed, apparently happy and well. He was furious with the doctor, who was mystified, saying he was certain the child had been dead.

This incident was to change Dorothy's life forever. She kept insisting to her parents that she wanted to 'go home', and when they told her that she was at home, she used to say, 'No, my *real* home.' At the age of four her parents took her to the British Museum, as they were taking relatives out for the day. They expected the child to be bored stiff with the statues and antiquities, but when she entered the Egyptian Department Dorothy became ecstatic and went running through the rooms, kissing the feet of the statues. When her parents told her it was time to go home, she implored them: 'Leave me, these are my people.'

Some time later Dorothy's father bought her a set of the *Children's Encyclopedia*, then an extremely popular reference guide for young people, thinking that maybe she would appreciate it when she was older. But even before she could read, Dorothy would pore over the entries and pictures about Ancient Egypt. She looked at the hieroglyphics on the pictures, and when her parents told her she couldn't possibly understand what the signs meant, she said: 'I do know it, but I've just forgotten it.'

Dorothy's parents decided that their daughter was extremely odd, and hoped she would grow out of her obsession with Ancient Egypt. But it grew and grew until she spent every single moment possible in the British Museum, studying the Egyptian relics. It was while she was staying on her grandmother's farm in Sussex that she began to have dreams, or visions, about her previous life in Ancient Egypt. She dreamed that a Pharaoh, Sety I, had come to her in the night, and she also had dreams of a strange underground hall somewhere in Egypt.

By the time Dorothy was sixteen, she was spending all her time reading about Ancient Egypt. She gradually became convinced that she had been, in a previous life, a lover of King Sety I. Bit by bit she pieced it together. In Ancient Egypt her name was Bentreshyt, and she was the daughter of a flower seller and a soldier. She had captured the heart of the king and had borne his son.

A little later the family moved to Plymouth, where Dorothy went to art school and attended a group which openly discussed the possibility of reincarnation. By this time she was convinced that reincarnation was a fact, and that in a past life she had lived in Ancient Egypt. Always open about her Egyptian connections, she consulted several spiritualists, who told her that the most likely explanation of her obsession was that at the age of three, when she fell, an ancient spirit had entered her body and was now controlling her. Dorothy dismissed this explanation and continued to study all she could about Egyptian antiquities.

At the age of twenty-seven, she got a job in London with an Egyptian magazine, for which she wrote articles and drew cartoons promoting the cause of Egyptian independence. When she was twenty-nine, she accepted a proposal of marriage from Imam Abdel Meguid, who was studying to be a teacher. In 1933 they sailed to Cairo, where Dorothy soon produced a son whom she called Sety. From then on Dorothy Eady became known as 'Omm Sety' – the mother of Sety – in accordance with Egyptian custom, by which a married woman is always called by the name of her eldest male child.

Dorothy never returned to England, and made Egypt her home, despite the fact that her marriage did not work out and in 1936 she was divorced. She was quite cheerful about this, saying to friends: 'I married the Egyptian Antiquities Department. So everybody was happy.' Dorothy was offered a job as a draughtswoman with the Department of Antiquities in Cairo, the very first woman ever to take such a job; she worked for Dr Selim Hassan, a world-famous Egyptologist of his time, and absorbed ever more information about Ancient Egypt. She herself became a leading Egyptologist and developed many professional skills, but there was always a 'peculiar side' to Dorothy. She did not like spending the night with anybody, because when she was in bed her lover Sety would come to her. Dorothy lived for these times. She was also very involved in astral projection and visions.

At first she took her son Sety to work with her, but later his father claimed him and she let him go without any fuss, saying: 'I've always preferred cats to children, anyway.' As might be expected, Dorothy soon became a 'character', known by all the tour operators, professors and keepers of museums. She had a quick and ready wit and appeared afraid of nothing. Once some women in Cairo shouted at her in the street, 'Go home, English whore!' and Dorothy immediately answered back: 'And leave all the customers to you?'

When she was fifty-two she decided it was time to fulfil her destiny and spend the rest of her days in Abydos, where as a temple priestess she had been the lover of Sety. She wished to continue her passionate affair with the king and felt she had to go to Abydos to do so, so she obtained a part-time job in the Department of Antiquities there. She lived in very primitive conditions, surrounding herself with cats, dogs and geese, but felt she had finally come 'home'. Dorothy spent as much time as possible in the Temple of Sety, where she offered herself as a guide to tourists and rapidly became famous.

When she first decided to live at Abydos, people asked if she wouldn't be afraid of the native Egyptians, who might not be very friendly. But in fact they became afraid of her, believing that she had magical powers. Dorothy herself fostered this belief by developing skills in herbal healing, and growing suitable herbs in the garden of her two-room mud-brick house.

She said once to Maureen Tracey, a tourist guide and author of a number of books on Egypt: 'You know, Tracey, people come here thinking they were once Cleopatra because they can see a picture of Anthony in their mind. They've all been Cleopatra and Hatsheput and Rameses and Thotmes. But they've never been a *nobody*! I was just one of the old scrubbers, I was nothing – the daughter of a soldier and a vegetable seller you know, who was left on the steps of the temple.' Dorothy told visitors that she didn't at all mind living alone, because Iris and Osiris were always hovering over her 'in one way or another'.

Dorothy Eady died in Abydos on 21 April 1981, leaving behind her a huge amount of written material of the Joan Grant variety – dream-like stories of her time as the lover of King Sety I.

As with most people who have publicly claimed past lives and reincarnation experiences, Dorothy Eady's diaries, experiences and stories have been subjected to intense scientific and psychological investigation. Unlike Joan Grant, who steadfastly refused to research her books in the normal way, saying that she preferred to rely on her 'far memory', Dorothy Eady consciously set out, from her earliest years, to become an expert Egyptologist. Some of her past-life memories led to important archaeological discoveries, which is why she is still so respected by her fellow Egyptologists today.

So she was not entirely peculiar, although her visions and astral projections, and her habits of sleepwalking and haunting the Temple of Sety at Abydos, gave her the reputation of a decided eccentric in her lifetime. But is Dorothy Eady's story one of true reincarnation – or is it a piecing together of some fantasy from her avid reading and studying of ancient Egyptian matters? Jonathan Cott, author of the latest book on Dorothy Eady, *The Search for Omm Sety*, mentions some 'for and against' theories which have been advanced to explain the phenomenon.

Biologist Lyall Watson, himself the author of a number of books on extremely odd subjects, believes that there is a simple non-reincarnationist answer to the story. His view is that there is vast untapped information in the genes, and that it is not at all odd that a three-year-old child might, in certain circumstances, inherit or acquire, and then organize, a second personality. 'The very scarcity of those with unusual knowledge or skill tends, I suggest, to support this biological explanation rather than that of reincarnation.'

In the American edition of *The Search for Omm Sety* the astronomer Carl Sagan commented:

Dorothy Eady was a lively, intelligent, dedicated woman who
made real contributions to Egyptology. This is true whether her

belief in reincarnation is fact or fantasy. In assessing the evidence, such as it is, we must recognise that many of us have a powerful predisposition to believe in life after death and in reincarnation. . . . Recognising that our hopes may make us vulnerable to self-deception, the burden of proof must clearly fall on the shoulders of those who claim there is evidence for reincarnation.

Sagan feels that the most logical explanation is that Dorothy carried strong childhood and adolescent fantasies about her past life in Egypt over into adulthood without 'sufficiently scrupulous attention to the boundary between fact and fantasy. I don't think we should be too hard on her,' he concluded, 'clearly what resulted was a far richer life than she might otherwise have had'.

This aspect is true, of course, for most of the people who have claimed past lives and have then acted on this belief. Joan Grant became world-famous for her 'far memory' books and, in later life, was considered something of an awesome sage. Certainly the life open to a woman of Dorothy Eady's social background in those days would not have been at all exciting.

The upshot of the 'expert' comments is that, although Omm Sety was undoubtedly a remarkable person who could not in any sense be dismissed simply as a crank, there is no real irrefutable evidence of reincarnation here. Dr Veronica Seton-Williams, an Egyptologist who knew her, remarked: 'You can't explain Omm Sety – she was a very strange creature.'

## The Thompson – Gifford case

This case is rather different from the ones described previously, as it is an example of involuntary supposed possession, or the taking over of a living person by a dead one. Like most of these matters, the Thompson-Gifford case has been subjected to an enormous amount of investigation. It is basically the story of how a young man appeared to be possessed by a dead painter, even painting in so close an approximation of his style that experts could not tell the difference.

The story starts in January 1907, when Frederic Thompson, then aged thirty-nine, arrived at the American Institute for Scientific Research in New York to say that he had been experiencing strange hallucinations of landscapes which he then felt compelled to paint. He added that he believed he was being possessed by a dead artist who had once lived in the same town of New Bedford, Massachusetts.

Thompson had met the artist, Robert Swain Gifford, about nine years previously, when both were out sketching along the coast. Gifford was then in his fifties and at the height of his fame. Thompson was at the time employed as a metalworker, but he had a small artistic talent that he was trying to develop in his spare time. Not long after Thompson first met Gifford he was made redundant from his job, and moved to New York where he set up in business as a silversmith. By 1905 Thompson had not seen Gifford for some years. The two men had never known each other well, and Thompson had no idea that on 15 January Gifford had died from a heart condition at the age of sixty-four.

Soon after this date, Thompson began to have an insatiable urge to paint and sketch. Although he had always been a keen amateur artist, this urge was different, as it was accompanied by strong mental images of trees and landscapes. Whenever Thompson sat down at his easel the pictures seemed to paint themselves, as if some unseen hand was guiding him. As time went on, Thompson remembered Gifford and seemed to have the impression that he was Gifford himself.

Thompson even told his wife that 'Mr Gifford' wanted to go sketching. During the whole of 1905 the urge to paint grew stronger and stronger, until in the end he gave up his silversmith's job and moved with his wife to Connecticut. He could no longer control the urges to paint and sketch and felt strongly that some force, not entirely welcome, was taking him over. Thompson said that he had heard a voice saying: 'Can you not take up and finish my work?'

Eventually Thompson decided he must seek help and made an appointment with the founder of the American Society for Psychical Research, Dr James Hyslop, who was also professor of ethics and logic at Columbia University. Thompson told Hyslop when they met that he was terrified of going insane. Hyslop felt at first that Thompson was undergoing some kind of personality disintegration, possibly caused by mental illness of some kind. He advised his patient to give up painting and try to get back to his jewellery work. In the meantime he arranged for Thompson to see Margaret Gaule, a professional psychic.

When Thompson went to see her, she said that she immediately sensed the presence of an artist in the room and felt that the spirit presence might have committed suicide. She also felt that the spirit had been suffering from rheumatism while in the physical body. As the sitting progressed, Miss Gaule began to communicate with the dead artist, and described landscapes of the kind painted by Gifford. After this, Hyslop took Thompson to another psychic, Mrs Minnie Soule, who soon made contact with an entity who claimed he was trying to influence the sitter. Mrs Soule then described many of Gifford's characteristics, as well as some clothing and a rug in his home.

After these sittings Thompson began to explore some haunts that had attracted Gifford as a painter, and made lots more sketches. He gave some of them to Hyslop, who, intrigued by the case, went to see Mrs Gifford and found that she could corroborate much of what had been said in Thompson's psychic sittings.

Three years after Gifford's death Thompson was painting in the complete style of the deceased artist – which an art critic confirmed – and was even making money from the sale of the paintings; an art critic confirmed that Gifford's style was coming through Thompson, apparently unaltered. Hyslop undertook further psychical research, and in the end became convinced that the painter R. Swain Gifford's memory and artistic skills had somehow transferred themselves to Thompson.

For his part Frederic Thompson continued to paint in the style of Gifford, and as late as 1922 was having exhibitions of psychically inspired paintings. After this date, the story of Frederic Thompson becomes obscure and facts are few. R Scott Rogo, an American psychologist and psychic researcher who has researched the Thompson-Gifford case thoroughly, believes he died somewhere between 1927 and 1935.

The Thompson – Gifford case has much in common with the story of London housewife Rosemary Brown in the sixties and seventies. Mrs Brown, no more than an average pianist, suddenly found that when she was sitting at the piano new music in the style of famous composers, such as Beethoven, Liszt and Mozart, was channelled through her. Her case was well documented and investigated.

## The Bloxham Tapes

The first documented examples of regression, the Bloxham Tapes of the 1970s, related the 'past lives' of a number of ordinary people, most of whom remained anonymous. Arnall Bloxham became interested in hypnotism while he was a schoolboy, after he had experienced dreams of what he came to believe were scenes in a past life. He later became a distinguished hypnotherapist and was able to regress his patients into past lives, mainly to cure phobic states and deep anxieties. Bloxham knew that under hypnosis people were often extremely suggestible, and were liable to embroider and fantasize information which they had acquired normally but which they had consciously forgotten. However, he was still convinced that some of his patients really did talk about their previous lives while under hypnosis. Bloxham said himself that most of the past lives described by his patients were extremely dull, which he felt was some kind of guarantee that they were genuine. His work and the stories of some of his more interesting subjects were the subject of a television documentary and a book, *More Lives Than One*, by Jeffrey Iverson. One story in particular, that of 'Jane Evans', has excited the attention of psychic researchers.

Jane Evans, a pseudonym for a Welsh housewife, agreed to be hypnotized by Bloxham, and under hypnosis described in varying detail about half a dozen past lives, some of which were exotic and out-of-the-ordinary. At various times Jane Evans was, she claimed, a Roman matron, a Jewess in York in the Middle Ages, a handmaid to Catherine of Aragon, and a nun in nineteenth-century America.

One of these supposed past incarnations, that of the Jewess in York, has been extensively investigated. 'Rebecca', the woman in question, lived in York in the twelfth century and was married with two children. Under hypnosis, Jane Evans was able to describe in remarkable detail her life at the time. She talked about the persecution of Jews in York at the time, and spoke about the family's flight to take refuge in the crypt of a church. Rebecca and one of her children hid in the crypt while her husband and other child went foraging for food. But the soldiers and mob found them and soon they were all killed.

Since there was so much to go on in this story, a lecturer at York University, Barrie Bodson, decided to look into it further. He discovered that the story was entirely true, that all the facts checked out and that the church described under hypnosis was quite clearly St Mary's in Castlegate. But there was no evidence for any kind of crypt.

However, six months after Jeffrey Iverson visited St Mary's for research on his book, a crypt was discovered by workmen as they were converting the former church into a museum. They described arches and vaults which were very similar to those mentioned by Jane Evans in her

'Rebecca' mode. Paranormal researcher Arthur Ellison, formerly professor of electrical and electronic engineering at the City University in London, says in his book *The Reality of the Paranormal*: 'It is important to note that Rebecca's story is not at all the history book version. Important facts of this history of the time are omitted and the whole gives an impression of an eye-witness rather than of someone fantasizing about material read earlier.'

Most people who believe in reincarnation as a reality feel that this story provides almost irrefutable confirmation that we may have lived before. However, another investigator, Ian Wilson, was not so sure. He wondered whether Jane Evans' stories could be in fact examples of cryptomnesia, rather than genuine stories of past lives, and he undertook his own researches. He went to see the woman – who was, he says, horrified that her cover had been blown and refused to talk to him, even though her story had been told on television.

Wilson, author of *Mind Out of Time*, which does all it can to debunk reincarnation, said: 'There seemed no possible way that Jane Evans could have known that the crypt was there. But when I went to see her she was horrified that I had discovered her whereabouts, and completely refused to discuss her past lives either with me, or anybody else.

'To me this suggests that somewhere deep inside herself she knows that the memories are not of genuine reincarnation. My explanation of the case is that "Jane Evans" had read a lot of historical novels, and that incidents from them had been locked into her unconscious. In fact, there is a historical novel in existence which describes such a crypt as "Rebecca" supposedly hid in. People often read historical novels and then completely forget that they have read them' Wilson said.

He added that he would like to believe in reincarnation – but has not so far found any convincing enough evidence of its reality.

## The work of Ian Stevenson

Sooner or later, anybody who undertakes any kind of investigation into reincarnation will come across the name of Ian Stevenson, a psychiatry professor who has researched the subject exhaustively all over the world and has written a number of books on the subject. Dr Stevenson, born in 1918, came from a theosophical background, so from an early age had an open mind on the subject. As an adult he became convinced that, if reincarnation did exist, it must be possible to prove it one way or the other. Since 1960 he has been collecting a huge number of cases 'of the reincarnation type', as he calls them, and his work has been praised for its scholarly and objective approach.

Although Dr Stevenson's name is well known to researchers, he remains a shadowy figure as far as the public are concerned. One reason is that he has steadfastly refused to give media interviews on his work, preferring to let his books speak for themselves. The trouble is that the books are long and academic rather than popular in tone, so they are relatively inaccessible to the general reader.

Dr Stevenson believes that the spontaneous memories of children offer the best evidence of reincarnation. He is dismissive of hypnosis, or hypnotic regression methods, believing that they leave the way wide open for suggestion, fantasizing and bringing buried memories to the surface. In other words, there is no real way of ever establishing whether the 'past lives' supposedly remembered under hypnosis are genuine or not. Small children, however, have not read historical novels, have not seen very much television and have not had much formal education at school. Therefore, according to Dr Stevenson, their memories are more likely to be unclouded by cryptomnesia.

Here are a few of the typical cases collected by Dr Stevenson, which now number around two thousand. They are taken from his latest book, *Children Who Remember Previous Lives*, published in 1987. He used no hypnosis, but relied on gentle questioning to draw the information from the child. In all the cases described, Dr Stevenson was able to corroborate the child's statements by talking to adults.

Gopal Gupta was born in Delhi on 26 August 1956. His parents were lower middle-class, and to them Gopal was a completely ordinary little boy. When he was about two and a half, however, his father asked him to remove a glass of water that a guest had used. Gopal replied: 'I won't pick it up. I am a Sharma' – that is, a member of India's highest caste, the Brahmins. Traditionally, Brahmins would not lower themselves to undertake a menial task such as picking up a used glass. The child then broke several glasses in temper.

Gopal's father asked him to explain why he had broken the glasses, and the little boy gave an astonishing explanation. He said that he had been the owner of a medical company called Sukh Shancharak and that he owned a large house. He also had a wife and two brothers, one of whom had shot and killed him. Gopal mentioned that he had lived in the city of Mathura, about three hundred miles south of Delhi.

Gopal's father was intrigued and mentioned the strange story to his friends, one of whom remembered that there had been a murder in Mathura. In 1964, when Gopal was nine, his father went to Mathura for a religious festival and discovered that there was indeed a Sukh Shancharak Company in existence. The sales manager there confirmed that one of the owners of the company had shot and killed his brother, another owner, on 27 May 1948.

The sales manager mentioned Gopal's story to the Sharma family, who then visited Gopal in Delhi and invited him to come and see them in Mathura. When he did so, he said he recognized several of the places and people. The Sharma family were impressed with the detail in Gopal's stories about them – he mentioned incidents that never came out in the story of the murder, which at the time was widely reported.

In his account of the case, Dr Stevenson remarks that all through his childhood Gopal behaved far more like a Brahmin than a member of his parents' caste. He would not undertake any housework, or drink milk from a cup which anybody else had used.

Dr Jamuna Prasad, who had worked with Dr Stevenson on reincarnation cases for many years, started investigating this case in 1965. Dr Stevenson became interested in it in 1969, and interviewed both families concerned. He remained in touch with the case until 1974, discovering that, as Gopal grew up, he lost all interest in the Sharma family and also gradually lost the traces of his former inappropriate Brahmin behaviour.

For Dr Stevenson, the story of Gopal is a strong one to support reincarnation, as the little boy could not have known anything about the murder case when he began to speak of it. It is true, says Stevenson, that Shaktipal Sharma, the murdered owner of the medical company, was a member of a prominent family in Mathura, and that his murder was a big story when it happened. But, says Stevenson, the Sharmas and the Guptas lived many miles apart and were from widely differing social backgrounds. Stevenson concludes: 'I have no hesitation in believing members of both families who said that they had never heard of the other family before the case developed.'

The next story comes from Upper Burma. Ma Tin Aung Myo was born in the village of Nathul on 26 December 1953. When her mother was pregnant, she had a dream of a Japanese soldier following her and saying that he would come to stay with her and her husband.

She thought no more of this until her daughter was three or four years old, when the little girl began to talk about having been a Japanese soldier.

Ma Tin Aung Myo told her mother that she had been a Japanese soldier stationed in Nathul during the Second World War, when the Japanese army had occupied Burma. She said that, as a soldier, her job was to cook. An Allied plane had killed her in the village.

There were also a few other details. Ma Tin said she came from the northern part of Japan and had been married with several children. Before becoming a soldier, she had been a shopkeeper. She was also able to describe what the Japanese soldier had been wearing, but she could not remember the name of the soldier or anybody connected with him. This meant that Dr Stevenson and his researchers could not check details with the Japanese family concerned.

They were, however, able to check general details about the Japanese in Nathul at the time in question. As a small child, Ma Tin behaved far more like a Japanese soldier than a Burmese girl. She showed a preference for Japanese food and frequently said she wanted to go back to Japan.

The most remarkable indication to Dr Stevenson was Ma Tin's extreme tomboyishness. She insisted on dressing in boys' clothes and having her hair cut short like a boy's. This caused problems at school, where Ma Tin was told to come dressed like a girl or else she would be expelled. She refused, and so her formal education stopped at the age of eleven. Dr Stevenson met Ma Tin in 1974 when she was working as a sandwich seller at a nearby railway station.

As a young child, he says, Ma Tin had always liked playing at soldiers, and as she grew up she assumed as masculine an identity as possible. She was very probably transsexual, as she said she never wanted to marry a man but to have a wife and be the 'man' of the family. It was clear that she considered herself basically male rather than female, although anatomically and biologically she was a completely normal female.

Her family came to accept that her unusual behaviour was caused by her previous incarnation as a Japanese soldier. (In fact, very many transsexuals believe that this is the real explanation of their problem: that in a previous life they were of the opposite sex, and that their previous gender has somehow remained in their memory, so that they cannot accept themselves in the current gender. Most reincarnationists accept that the soul, or spirit, is neuter and can inhabit both male and female bodies in successive incarnations. Several of Joan Grant's books are about previous incarnations in a male body.)

Another case thoroughly investigated by Dr Stevenson is that of Samuel Helander, who was born in Helsinki, Finland, on 15 April 1976. Finland, of course, unlike the Far East, does not officially accept the concept of reincarnation. Before Samuel was two years old he began talking about his mother's younger brother, Perrti Hailio, who had died of diabetes in 1975, aged eighteen. This caused great upset to his family, for when Samuel's mother Marja had been pregnant with him, she had had a dream about her brother. Apparently she had been considering an abortion, but in her dream she heard her brother say quite clearly, 'Keep that child.'

Soon after Samuel began to speak, he announced that his name was 'Pelti' (the nearest he could get to Perrti) and refused to answer to Samuel. When he saw a photograph of Perrti as a young child in a baby walker, Samuel stated that the child was himself, and that he had been taken to hospital with his legs in plaster. Nothing in the photograph indicated that the legs had been in plaster, but in fact the young Perrti's legs had both been fractured in an accident. Every time Samuel saw pictures of Perrti in a photograph album he would shout: 'That's me!' Samuel was also able to identify several objects which had belonged to Perrti – a guitar, a jacket, a watch. And when he was taken to the cemetery where Perrti had been buried, he looked at the grave and said: 'This is my grave.'

As he grew up, Samuel exhibited a severe phobia about water. One of the symptoms of diabetes is an uncontrollable thirst, and this had been noticed in the young Perrti – although at the time nobody realized just how ill he really was. The boy also exhibited several physical characteristics of Perrti's, such as the habit of standing with one foot forward and his hand on his hip. Dr Stevenson notes that no other members of the family stood like this, so Samuel could not have picked it up from anybody.

The final case from Dr Stevenson's book that I want to discuss is that of Susan Eastland. The information came from Susan's mother, Charlotte Eastland, who became certain that her daughter had unusual memories of her older sister Winnie, who had been killed in a car crash in 1961 at the age of six. Two years later Mrs Eastland became pregnant again, and Susan was born in 1964. During her pregnancy she had dreamed that Winnie was back in the family; in fact, in the delivery room Mr Eastland distinctly thought he heard Winnie's voice saying: 'Daddy, I'm coming home.'

So the Eastlands were already attuned to the idea that the new baby, Susan, might in fact be Winnie reborn to them, despite the fact that the family background was not one to encourage any kind of belief in reincarnation – very much the reverse, in fact, as Mrs Eastland had belonged to a church which strongly taught against such a possibility. She also assured Dr Stevenson that until 1969 she had never told any of her children – there were two others called Richard and Sharon – about her conviction that Winnie had come to them again in the form of Susan.

When Susan was about two years old, she started to make remarks which indicated she had some connection with her dead sister. When asked her age, Susan would reply that she was six years old. She also expressed interest in photographs of Winnie, insisting: 'That was me.' On one occasion she wrote letters on the kitchen door which spelled WINNI, and talked about 'When I was at school', even though she had not yet been to school. She also spoke of events in which Winnie had participated, such as going to the beach on an outing and correctly naming several of the other people who were there.

Mrs Eastland told Dr Stevenson that Susan shared much of Winnie's personality, saying that both were rather aggressive girls and very well co-ordinated for their age. Susan did not look at all like Winnie, but had a small birthmark on her left hip in the place where Winnie had received her fatal injury. (Dr Stevenson places importance on this kind of birthmark.)

He admits that these cases – and many others like them – do not prove conclusively one way or the other that reincarnation exists, or that children can spontaneously remember previous lives. He also admits that most of the cases he has studied in detail occur outside Western culture, where the whole subject of reincarnation is much more accepted.

Of course, his work raises very many questions, of which the uppermost is probably this. Even though Dr Stevenson has collected many hundreds of cases, they still only represent a tiny proportion of the children in the world. Statistically, the numbers are insignificant. So why do so few children appear to have any recollection at all of a previous life? Dr Stevenson says: 'Remembering previous lives is an unusual experience that occurs to only a few people for reasons we are only just beginning to understand.' The main problem with the whole subject, he says, is that it cannot be studied scientifically. There can be no laboratory tests, no double-blind controlled trials, no irrefutable evidence that these children really have lived before. Even where cases have checked out well, there remains the distinct possibility that parents are making it up, that it is all wishful thinking, that the child has unknowingly overheard conversations. Another possibility, supported by cynical researchers such as Ian Wilson, is that the parents might have put their children up to it. This is especially likely in India, where most of the cases are of children being reborn into a poorer or lower-caste family, who might hope to receive largesse from the earlier, richer family.

While keeping an open mind on the subject, Dr Stevenson suggests that several 'unexplained' aspects of life can become clear when one accepts the possibility of reincarnation. It may explain unusual behaviour which currently baffles psychologists and psychiatrists, such as severe phobias which have no discernible root cause. In the cases Dr Stevenson has studied, children often showed severe phobias of water, fire, snakes and so on long before they learned to speak. The appearance of birthmarks in the very places where the previous person sustained a fatal accident would also be explained by reincarnation.

The question of the child prodigy has often been advanced to give evidence of reincarnation, and Dr Stevenson discusses this. In the family of Handel, for instance, there were no known ancestors with an interest in music. Elizabeth Fry, the prison reformer, and Florence Nightingale both developed high-achieving careers totally against the wishes of their family – both felt called to their vocations, and nothing whatever could stop them from following the call. There is at the moment no genetic or biological explanation to account for unusual aptitudes or untaught skills, even though so far no child prodigy has ever attributed special skills to a previous life. The children studied by Ian Stevenson have been extremely ordinary and not precocious in any way. As they grew up, they gradually forgot that they had once been 'other people', and settled down to mundane lives.

The still unexplained phenomenon of transsexualism, where physically normal boys and girls are somehow convinced that they are really of the opposite gender, but somehow housed in the wrong kind of body, becomes more explicable in the light of reincarnation, suggests Stevenson. He has on record a large number of cases of persistent gender confusion, which always starts when the child is very young and leads them to reject their anatomical bodies as they grow older. Unlike other memories of previous lives this conviction does not fade, but rather grows stronger with age. Transsexualism has been observed in every culture and race and has nothing to do with whether boys are the more preferred sex, or whether parents wanted a child of a particular gender and were disappointed with what they got.

So, Stevenson asks, why doesn't every child remember a previous life? There are several possible answers here. One is that there is no evidence at all that everybody has a previous life anyway. For some, this may be their first incarnation on earth. This explanation would tie up with the account given by Sister Jayanti of the Brahma Kumaris, who says that new souls are coming into incarnation all the time, and that for many this birth would be their first one.

One possible reason why Dr Stevenson's cases remember past lives is that many of them had untimely deaths, and were therefore in a state of incompleteness when they died. There is a high incidence of violent death, by murder or fatal accident, and most of the previous lives were young at the time of death. 'At the times of death they might have felt entitled to a longer life, and may have generated a craving for rebirth perhaps leading to a quicker reincarnation', Stevenson writes.

Dr Stevenson quickly dismisses the idea that the children claiming to remember previous lives were seeking special treatment, or to mark themselves out in some way. In very many cases the reverse was true – the children have not been understood, their behaviour has been regarded as abnormal, and the children themselves have felt that nobody understands them. In most cases, in fact, remembering the previous life has not been in any way beneficial to the child concerned. Furthermore, the memories are likely to be of unpleasant, rather than pleasant events, so there is really little incentive for the child to talk about a previous life.

Dr Stevenson concludes his examination of the evidence for reincarnation – which will be discussed more fully in Chapter 6, along with other claimed evidence for and against – by saying that we know almost nothing about reincarnation, and still have to rely largely on assertion, mainly by religious and spiritual groups. He does say, however, that in world terms the belief that we only have one physical life is very much a minority concept. The numbers of people in the world who accept reincarnation as a fact are far greater than those who dismiss it as primitive superstition.

## T Lobsang Rampa

This section would not be complete without a word on T Lobsang Rampa, the supposed Tibetan monk who between about 1957 and 1967 wrote a dozen or so books about *karma* and reincarnation, astral travel, levitation and developing psychic powers. His first and most famous book was *The Third Eye*, which is supposed to be the autobiography of a Tibetan lama, one of the 'few who have reached this strange Western world'. In fact T – for Tuesday, designating the day of the week on which he was born – Lobsang Rampa had never been to Tibet in his life, but was a Devonshire farmer's son by the name of Albert Price. Before he hit on the idea of calling himself Lobsang Rampa he was known as Dr Karl Ku'An, a doctor of medicine from China.

When *The Third Eye* appeared on the scene, with its vivid descriptions of life in a Tibetan monastery, it became an instant bestseller. Not long after publication, however, Lobsang Rampa became involved in a sordid court case in which he was 'exposed'. But he went on writing books – and the public lapped them up.

Read with hindsight, *The Third Eye* has a curious air of unreality. It tells of how Rampa, who came from a millionaire's family in Tibet, went into a monastery at the age of seven, and then was taught to develop and use special powers with the aid of the 'third eye', which was a hole in his forehead gouged out of the skin and bone with a miniature chainsaw and then plugged with treated wood until it had healed. Rampa talks about the concept of reincarnation like this:

> It all seemed very hard, the severity of the teachers. But then, I
> consoled myself, that is why I came, to learn. That is why I
> reincarnated, although then I did not remember what it was that
> I had to relearn. We firmly believe in reincarnation, in Tibet.
> We believe that when one reaches a certain stage of evolution,
> one can choose to go on to another plane of existence, or return
> to earth to learn something more, or to help others. It may be
> that a wise man had a certain mission in life, but died before he
> could complete his work. In that case, so we believe, he can
> return to complete his task, providing that the result will be of
> benefit to others. Very few people could have their previous
> incarnations traced back, there had to be certain signs and the
> cost and time would prohibit it. Those who had those signs, as I
> had, were termed 'Living Incarnations'. They were subjected to
> the sternest of stern treatment when they were young – as I had
> been – but became objects of reverence when they became
> older. In my case I was going to have special treatment, to 'force
> feed' my occult knowledge. Why, I did not know, then!

T Lobsang Rampa went to great lengths to try to make his 'autobiography' sound authentic, and in his preface does his best to make the story seem a first-hand account. He relates how he was taken to communist China when the Chinese invaded Tibet, and then escaped somehow to England. 'Some of my statements, so I am told, may not be believed. That is your privilege, but Tibet is a country unknown to the rest of the world.' He goes on to say that many people who told of fantastic things in the past were disbelieved, although they were later found to be truthful and accurate. 'So will I be' ends T Lobsang Rampa.

He must have thought that nobody would ever be able to check up on what he said, but just a few years later Dr Michael Dillon – the first biological woman to have a sex-change operation and live as a man – was ordained a Buddhist monk in Ladakh, next to Tibet, and so learned at first hand what life in a Tibetan monastery was like. It bore little relation to the existence that Lobsang Rampa had described. But Dr Dillon, who met Rampa in 1957, said that the man definitely possessed psychic and occult powers, but that he could levitate or go on astral travels, as he maintained in *The Third Eye*, was unlikely.

The strange thing is that, when Lobsang Rampa was exposed as a fake, his books became even more popular. Although we can discount 'The Autobiography of a Tibetan Lama', as he subtitled *The Third Eye*, he did know a great deal about Eastern religions, and many of his later philosophical books dispense handy wisdom. Rampa received thousands of letters from readers, asking him whether his experiences were really true and how they should conduct their lives. All of his books deal with the reality of *karma* and reincarnation; for example in one of his last, *Chapters of Life*, he writes:

> Quite a number of people are brought together to work out
> karmic links, and the working out of these karmic ties makes it
> necessary that people shall come in close contact with each other
> for good or for bad. If a man and a woman are brought together
> through karmic ties and, for example, the man falls in love with
> the woman and the woman falls in love with the man, then a
> very great bond of love is formed which can have the effect of
> cancelling out many bad karmic aspects, because no matter what
> we think down here, good will prevail in the end.

He goes on:

> Any reaction to any other person starts the chain which causes
> karma. For example, there can be a relationship between a
> teacher and a student, in that case a bond of some sort is formed.
> It could be a lasting bond, or it may be just a temporary bond
> which is over almost in a flash and can then be attributed to the
> burning out of some karmic link.

# Many Lives, Many Masters

This book, by psychiatrist Brian Weiss, is about the many supposed previous lives of a seventeen-year-old patient whom he calls Catherine. Dr Weiss, currently chief of psychiatry at the University of Miami, describes how the experience of taking her back through her previous lives changed his own life and outlook. Catherine, who worked as a laboratory technician, suffered from many phobias and irrational fears; she also had regular panic attacks but could never pinpoint the cause.

At first Dr Weiss took her back to her early childhood, but soon discovered that the phobias did not begin then. Although she remembered a number of unpleasant incidents from that time, all her fears and vivid nightmares remained intact. Dr Weiss wondered if there might be something odd about her case when one day she visited a museum of Egyptian antiquities with her boyfriend and seemed to know all about the exhibits. She agreed to undergo hypnotic regression, in which she remembered events further and further back. But Dr Weiss was, he says, totally unprepared for what came next.

Under hypnosis, Catherine became 'Aronda', aged eighteen and mentioned the year 1863. Still Aronda, she then became twenty-five years old with a child called 'Cleastra'. Catherine said of Cleastra, 'She's Rachel' – her young niece in this incarnation. At this time a flood was devastating the village, and Aronda perished in it. Dr Weiss writes: 'My clinical mind told me she was not fantasizing this material, that she was not making it up.' He mentions that he ran through the gamut of possible psychiatric disorders which might explain her condition – hallucinations, schizophrenia, delusions, multiple personality. None seemed to fit.

It seemed that as soon as one fear disappeared – Catherine's severe water phobia vanished when the 'Aronda' incarnation was dredged up from the unconscious – another one came in its place. During subsequent hypnosis sessions Catherine remembered many more previous lives, including one in Ancient Greece, where Brian Weiss, then Diogenes (although not the famous Stoic) was her teacher. Altogether Catherine went through dozens of incarnations, in many countries and of both sexes. After a time she herself became psychic, had precognitive dreams and also spoke of the 'Masters' – the same people, presumably, whom Helena Blavatsky managed to contact for her revelations. 'The Masters' told Catherine that she had so far incarnated eighty-six times. Many of these lives had ended in violent deaths, which appeared to be the cause of the many phobias and fears.

Catherine never claimed to be anybody famous in her past lives, which according to Dr Weiss gives all the more credence to what she was saying. He taped all the hypnotic utterances and records that when 'the Masters' were speaking through Catherine, they spoke in a style and with a wisdom that was quite different from anything she said in her waking state.

In the end, Dr Weiss states in his book, he had no choice but to accept the truth of what was being revealed through Catherine's hypnosis – that there is such a thing as reincarnation, that there are 'higher beings' on an 'astral plane', and that we have to come back to earth to complete unfinished business from the previous incarnation. He writes:

> My life has changed almost as drastically as Catherine's. I have become more intuitive, more aware of the hidden, secret parts of my patients, colleagues and friends. I seem to know a great deal about them, even before I should. My values and life goals have shifted to a more humanistic, less accumulative focus. Psychics, mediums, healers and others appear in my life with increasing frequency and I have started to systematically evaluate their abilities. . . . I have begun to meditate, something that, until recently, I thought only Hindus and Californians practised.

## Lee Ward

'When I look at people I can read their karmic record' says Lee Ward, the Kent housewife who described my three past lives with which this book began. I can see it just like a video. I have always had this ability, and even as a small child I seemed to be able to see things that other people couldn't. Of course, I didn't understand what it was then but now I do.

'I'm not a formal therapist, but I can often help people who are going through difficulties in their lives, or who have strange phobias that can't be cured by ordinary means. I don't use hypnosis; I don't need to.

'Most people I meet,' says Lee, 'are extremely sceptical when they first come to see me. But then, very often, they will hear something about themselves that will ring a bell, that will shake them and make them think again.'

Lee Ward says that all her information about people's past lives comes from having the ability to read the 'Akashic records', which played such a large part in theosophy. But why should she possess the ability to see into previous lives when most of us can't even begin to for a minute?

She says: 'I believe I've earned it through my own *karma*. I can now help people through this ability. Very often, people come to see me and say quite openly: "I don't believe in all this past life stuff, you know." I then say, "I don't care whether you believe or not, you still have experienced very many incarnations."'

'People often try to catch me out. Once I described a man's previous life in Russia, and he said that he didn't believe me for one minute. Then he read up in a library what I had told him and was staggered at how close it was to the truth, even down to the description of a stained glass window.

'I feel strongly that my ability has come out and is being used because the time is right. We are in the Age of Aquarius and people need to know the truth. The established church has lost its way and people are not finding what they need from orthodox religion. I am being used as a channel, and believe I can tell people whatever they need to hear. So many people feel so desperate these days and don't know what they want out of life.

'Many women, for instance, say they are desperate for a child if they find themselves infertile. When I see people like this, I delve into their past lives to see why they are so desperate, because really you can't be desperate for something you haven't got or have never had. Sometimes they've had eight children in a previous life and have enjoyed them, and they are unconsciously remembering this.

'Lots of people also want to find their ideal partners. But the idea that everyone has an ideal partner, a Mr or Miss Right, is nonsense. Relationships are breaking up fast because people form unsuitable liaisons in their fear of being alone. But some of us are meant to be alone. Looking into past lives can hold the key to so many present problems, and give valid answers. But if we do find ourselves marrying the wrong person, it's all to do with repaying past *karma*. Once that has been paid, the marriage can be dissolved and there need be no further business between the partners.

'I sometimes wonder why I'm here at all', Lee Ward said. 'I know that I belong at home – that is, on the non-physical plane. This material plane is an illusion and the reality is the non-physical.'

Most, if not all, of us, find the idea of 'past lives' fascinating, in the same way that even the most convinced sceptics will sneak a look at their horoscopes in newspapers or magazines. The very fact that researchers and scientists have been prepared to put so much effort into trying to establish whether these past lives are 'genuine' shows how seriously they are taken. Perhaps one day science will let us know in some irrefutable way whether 'past lives' are truly fact or fiction, but for the time being we have to reserve judgment. Even though some of the claimed previous lives have been exposed as fakes, and the stories of T Lobsang Rampa proved to be the most outrageous fabrications, not all can be dismissed so easily. Nobody has ever come forward to dismiss the 'far memory' of Joan Grant, and there has never been a satisfying neurological explanation of the Thompson – Gifford case. It is hard to explain many of Dr Ian Stevenson's cases as mere fabrication or fantasy. And although, according to Ian Wilson, the supposed past lives of 'Jane Evans' *could* have been cryptomnesic memories, the question remains, *were they?*

# CHAPTER FIVE

# *Near death, out-of-the-body and supernatural experiences*

Until the beginning of the nineteenth century it was assumed by many people that, in addition to a physical world that could be seen, touched and heard, there also existed a spirit world which was just as real in its own way. Then the new breed of Victorian scientist, who began to insist on observable proof for everything, began to shed serious doubt on this so-called 'spirit world'. If we couldn't see, hear or touch spirits, how could we possibly know that they existed? Proof now began to be demanded of things which had previously not seemed to need proof – communicating with the dead, non-physical aspects of human beings, the existence of ghosts, survival after death. It was no longer enough that these things should be a matter of faith or religious belief – they had to be *proved*.

For a long time, of course, there was no way of proving beyond all possible doubt that some part of us survived after death, perhaps for ever, perhaps to be reborn in another body, perhaps to live on the astral plane. Because of this lack of any kind of objective proof, belief in spirit entities died down and, in many cases, out. As the twentieth century progressed, fewer and fewer people were willing to believe in apparitions, ghosts, souls and spirits. Where, educated people kept asking, is the evidence?

Yet at the same time as firm belief in such things waned, the 'ghost industry', in the shape of horror films, became bigger than ever. Films such as *Rosemary's Baby*, *The Exorcist* and *The Amityville Horror* pulled in huge audiences all over the Western world. Although our rational minds may have told us there was no such thing as the supernatural, our emotions and imaginations weren't so convinced. And even those who profess most loudly that there are no such things as ghosts or supernatural happenings would hesitate to spend the night in an allegedly haunted house. Even the most rational and unemotional person could not be *absolutely* sure that there is no such thing.

# Near-death experiences

But now, those rational and non-religious people who have maintained that there is no such thing as a human spirit or soul, nothing which exists outside the material brain and body, are having to rethink their ideas. For recent research into what has come to be called the near-death experience suggests very strongly that humans do possess an aspect which has definite reality but which is not part of our physical body. Although there is still no proof that we may reincarnate, there is now sufficient scientific evidence available to suggest that, at the very least, there exists some part of us which is not merely a part of the physical body, but which has some kind of survival outside it. There is now a respectable body of evidence for some kind of survival after death.

This evidence has been obtained in two different ways. The Society for Physical Research, which for over a century has been investigating the so-called 'paranormal', has now amassed an impressive amount of evidence which should convince even the most sceptical that 'spirits' of some sort do exist. The other evidence, even harder to ignore, derives from the study of what has come to be called the near-death experience, or NDE. This phenomenon, which has now been studied by doctors and scientists all over the world, occurs when people are thought to be dead and then come back to life. Until the invention of resuscitation and life-support machines, researchers had to rely on anecdotal evidence of NDEs; now, though, people whose hearts have stopped have been brought back to life by sophisticated machinery, and have described what has happened when they were 'dead'. Almost all have a virtually identical experience, and this experience has been carefully examined.

The first popular book on NDEs was by Dr Raymond Moody, a former philosophy lecturer who later qualified as a medical doctor; he published his now famous *Life After Life* in 1975, after eleven years of extensive research into the subject. This book, which has been a bestseller on both sides of the Atlantic, describes the many cases investigated by Dr Moody and offers some conclusions; it also brings home to the reader just how similar most NDEs are. The subject of NDEs has been further studied in America by Professor Kenneth Ring, the author of a number of books on the subject.

In Britain, a great deal of work on NDEs has been carried out by psychologist Margot Grey, who herself experienced the near-death phenomenon in 1976. It was this which led her to undertake the first scientific study of the subject in the UK. Margot Grey was also a founder member of the International Association for Near-Death Studies (IANDS) which collects case histories and continues to amass data on this new field of research.

In the preface to her book *Return from Death* Margot Grey described her own near-death experience, which occurred while she was travelling in India:

> At some point during the process of passing in and out of
> consciousness I became aware that if I somehow urged myself I
> could rise up out of my body and remain in a state of levitation
> up against the ceiling in a corner of the room. At the time this
> seemed entirely natural and felt very pleasant and extremely
> freeing. I remember looking down at my body lying on the bed
> and feeling completely unperturbed by the fact that it seemed
> likely that I was going to die in a strange country half a world
> away from home, family and friends, and thinking it was really
> totally unimportant where I left my body, which I felt had served
> me well and like a favourite but worn-out coat had at last
> outlived its usefulness and would now have to be discarded.

After this, Margot Grey experienced what has come to be known as a typical NDE: she felt herself floating in total darkness in what seemed to be outer space, but she was not afraid and did not feel lonely. After this there was a sensation of travelling down a long tunnel, at the end of which was a point of light. She felt herself moving towards this light and, as she got nearer, her sense of exultation increased. She remembers feeling very close to the source of life and love, and embraced feelings of bliss, not fear. It was like being rapturously in love.

Margot Grey lived to tell the tale, and to hear many thousands of other people's tales about the near-death experience. She returned from India, and from death, to research a PhD in the near-death experience. She is now convinced that the NDE offers the most conclusive proof yet that the mind and personality are basically non-physical and are not part of the body. During a typical NDE, she says, people have thoughts and emotions. They are also able to reflect on their condition. But, commonly, they seem to have left their bodies far behind. Yet they still exist, in their minds at least, as whole people.

'The idea that life continues in some form or another after death is central to almost every major religious tradition throughout the world', she says in her book. All religions, without exception, hold that physical death is not the end of existence but before the advent of scientific research on NDEs we more or less had to accept this on trust. Now, however, she says, we can know. Near-death experiences have been reported by people of all religions, and of no religion at all. The NDE is just as likely to happen to an atheist as to a fervent believer in life after death.

People who have 'died' and then been resuscitated have commonly described five main elements in their NDE:

Peace and a sense of wellbeing;

Separation from the body;

Entering the darkness;

Seeing the light;

Entering the light.

These five elements have become known as the 'core' experience, and appear to be almost completely universal in that they cross all cultures, age groups and belief systems.

It has been commonly believed by spiritualists, mediums and sensitives, and others who purport to be able to communicate with the physically dead, that after bodily death people become much wiser and gain an ability to see things much more as they really are. Those of us who have so far been unable to communicate with spirits have had to take it on trust that Auntie Gladys in the spirit world has suddenly become a sage, when she uttered only platitudes in her bodily existence. This post-death wisdom has, in fact, been one of the stumbling-blocks about spiritualism and people have often asked: how is it that these ordinary people gain the ability to dispense universal wisdom once they pass over? The sneaking suggestion has always been, of course, that the medium is making it up and is not really communicating with Auntie Gladys or Uncle Bill at all. Of course, messages from the spirit world are often trivial and banal in the extreme. Mediums frequently explain this by saying that, although apparently unimportant, the messages will have significance to those for whom they are intended.

But the study of NDEs sheds light on this curious phenomenon. In her studies of the subject, Margot Grey discovered that after an NDE people are never the same again. They come back with a sense of spirituality, an altered perspective, increased wisdom. Those who have returned from death become more loving, more compassionate, less materially oriented and with a sense of having experienced some kind of spiritual rebirth. Again, this phenomenon is universally reported among people who have undergone NDEs and lends credence to the possibility that people do alter for the better once they have shed their physical overcoats. They also seem to 'come back' with psychic and special gifts which enable them to interpret what is going on around them and to predict future events – in other words they have gained an ability for extra-sensory perception which they did not have before the near-death experience. Some patients have reported that after their NDE they appear to have become clairvoyant; others have said that they now seem to be in possession of some absolute knowledge, and know of things they could not possibly have learned in books, and some NDErs develop the ability to produce automatic writing.

From what I have said so far it may seem as if I accept the NDE as scientific fact, rather than regarding it as a nice idea which is still awaiting evaluation. But after reading all the evidence, I feel I have no choice: the huge amount of scientific material on NDEs which has now been collected is overwhelmingly persuasive. Of course there *may* be a genetic, biochemical or neurological explanation of the whole phenomenon; so far, though, no one has offered a satisfactory alternative to the 'spirit' explanation.

Doctors and scientists who may have been sceptical of the work of Margot Grey, Dr Raymond Moody and Professor Kenneth Ring would have been startled to read some years ago in the *Lancet* of the near-death experience of an eminent professor, who was brought back from 'death' by a resuscitation machine and lived to write about it in this highly respectable medical journal. His original article was anonymous, but a Sunday news-paper, the *Mail on Sunday*, tracked him down and interviewed him about the experience.

The professor, who was very old and ill and in fact died soon after the article was published, described it as an extremely positive, even blissful experi-ence, and he remembered being unwillingly dragged back to life by nurses in the hospital. He had a very strong feeling that he did not want to come back, but would have preferred to stay in the new regions he had just entered.

It was impossible to say that the professor had not undergone these experiences, for he clearly had. But what could be the explanation? Scientific investigators of the NDE have explored all possible avenues – could the experience be a kind of defence mechanism to protect one from the reality of death? Could the NDE be caused by anaesthetic – after all, many drugs do induce altered perception – or could it be the result of lack of oxygen to the brain? Might there be a neurological explanation, such as temporal lobe seizure of the kind experienced by epileptics?

In some cases these factors might well apply, but the consensus of opinion is that they do not fit all NDEs by any means. There is good evidence that anaesthetics interfere with NDEs and that anaesthetized patients rarely have any recall afterwards. In any case, by no means all of those experiencing NDEs are under anaesthetic at the time. It is just possible that there may be a neurological explanation, says Kenneth Ring, as there has not yet been enough research on this aspect to rule it out for certain. As yet, though, there are too many differences between the genuine NDE and temporal lobe seizure for this explanation to be given much credence. The research so far undertaken on NDEs has made all biological and psychological explanations unlikely – they simply don't fit.

On the other hand, when one shifts perspective and considers the possibility of a paranormal explanation, the whole thing seems to make more sense. There is commonly precognition and a complete collapse of the usual sense of time. Patients who have been brought back from the brink of death have no idea how long they were 'dead'. The experience is much more like a dream than anything else, and recent scientific investigation appears to confirm what was written centuries ago in *The Tibetan Book of the Dead*, which describes an interval of suspension after we die that corresponds very closely to the sensations described by NDErs.

From what has been said so far, it would seem that all NDEs are extremely positive experiences which vastly improve the understanding and perception of those who have had them. But, says Margot Grey, this is not always the case. Although the overwhelming majority of NDEs *are* positive and blissful, some are extremely negative and frightening. In her book she described a number of 'negative' NDEs, in which the person experiences something much more like the traditional picture of Hell. Although such experiences are infrequently reported, they do exist and the few cases on record describe a feeling of loneliness and sense of desolation. There are descriptions of a dark and gloomy environment and a feeling of being on the brink of some horrible abyss. 'Some people', writes Margot Grey, 'felt that they were being tricked into death and needed to keep their wits about them to prevent this from happening.' But although some individuals do appear to have had negative experiences, they come back with a similar resolution to those who have had an enjoyable NDE – a conviction that physical life is not all, that they must modify their way of life and try to be better people in future, and that they have somehow been given a glimpse into an alternative reality.

Like the positive NDE, the negative experience has five basic constituents, which are:

Fear and a feeling of panic;

Out-of-the-body experience;

Entering a black void;

Sensing an evil force;

Entering a Hell-like environment.

In all cases of NDE studies, both positive and negative, there is an overwhelming feeling that the person was not ready to die, that his or her time had not yet come, and that there was unfinished business to complete. The conviction was that, once this business had been attended to, bodily death unaccompanied by resuscitation could occur. All those who have undergone NDEs remarked on how the experience had lessened their fear of death. They knew now that it was not the end, only another kind of beginning.

Margot Grey concludes her study thus: 'The idea that life continues after death varies of course with different cultures and ideologies, but basically what they are all saying is that death is not the end of existence, that in a different form consciousness continues after the body is no longer vital.

She goes on to make it clear that the NDE offers no kind of proof for a continuing life after death, as 'not one of the respondents went further than surviving the initial stages of death'. All that the case histories indicate is that consciousness seems to be in some way separate from the body. It can continue when vital organs, such as the heart, are no longer functioning, and when the subject has been declared 'brain dead'.

There also seems little doubt that NDEs are on the increase – possibly because of the sophisticated machinery now available to get hearts working again after an electrocardiogram reading shows that they have stopped. This new technology offers a unique opportunity to study in a clinical way one of the great unknowns of all time.

## Other evidence for survival after death

The other main avenue of research into the continuation of consciousness after physical death is that of the Society for Psychical Research, whose members have conducted a large number of exhaustive investigations into allegations of ghosts, spirit manifestations, apparitions, mediumship, communication with the dead through ouija boards, automatic writing, planchette, and so on.

Because the reports of most SPR research are so meticulous and exhaustive they often make quite boring reading, even when describing the most blood-curdling apparitions and experiences. Brian Inglis, one of the best-known writers on paranormal matters, has said: 'Anybody who elects to conduct research into apparitions consequently faces two hazards, if he undertakes fieldwork. "Ghosthunting" is immensely time-consuming and for the most part intensely boring; sitting around, often in the dark, waiting for something to happen with no certainty that anything will happen.'

Then there is the further complication that eye-witness accounts cannot be taken at face value. Unless the ghost or apparition is seen by an impartial observer, there can be no certainty that there was any supernatural phenomenon. Nevertheless, through the most profound scepticism, often on the part of the researchers themselves, there remains a handful of cases which cannot be explained by ordinary means. Perhaps they offer no absolute proof of some kind of survival after death, but there is no other satisfactory explanation for the following cases, which have been sifted and sifted again and examined from every angle by huge numbers of psychical researchers.

The first is the case of 'Feda', an entity supposedly from the spirit world, who manifested herself on many occasions to a professional medium, Mrs Gladys Osborne Leonard. Feda emerged when Mrs Leonard was in a trance state, and proceeded to convey information that Mrs Leonard could certainly not have received in any ordinary way. This was established in test after test: Mrs Leonard was put through the most rigorous investigations by SPR researchers of the time, and was pronounced genuine by Sir Oliver

Lodge, an early psychic researcher who was appointed principal of Birmingham University in 1900. Sir Oliver became convinced of Feda's reality when he tried to communicate with his youngest son Raymond, who had been killed at Ypres in September 1915.

Further confirmation was provided of Feda's powers by the novelist Radclyffe Hall, who was persuaded to make an appointment with Mrs Leonard after her long-time lover, Mabel Batten, died. Though sceptical at first, Radclyffe Hall was later in no doubt that her dead lover had come through. Her account of the sittings is well documented in her diaries and journals.

Andrew MacKenzie, who has, according to Brian Inglis, become the 'leading authority on apparitions', has devoted decades to investigating apparitions. In his preface to *Hauntings and Apparitions*, published to commemorate the centenary of the SPR in 1982, he says:

> A normal explanation for an experience must first be sought before we accept a paranormal one. All too often what is thought to be a ghost is in fact a living person. Sometimes there is a physical explanation for what seems to be a ghostly event. For instance, mist figures are frequently mistaken for ghosts, with the observer interpreting a grey or white shape as that of a nun or monk. However, this said, there are a great many cases in which the inescapable conclusion is, in my opinion, that the figure seen was that of an apparition, although we are unable to explain satisfactorily, in the light of present knowledge, what is involved in such an experience.

One of the most convincing cases of all time, according to MacKenzie, is that of Johnny Minney, who died at the age of five in 1921 and was subsequently 'seen' in a room on the farm where he had been born, at a village called Waresley, near Cambridge. It all happened in 1965 when an Australian woman, Stella Herbert, went to stay with a friend, Shirley Ross, also an Australian, who was at the time living at Vicarage Farm where Johnny Minney had been born and died. When she arrived, Mrs Herbert was introduced to Margaret Minney, who was Johnny's sister and had lived on the farm all her life.

On her first night at the farm, Mrs Herbert was woken up by a little boy kneeling at the side of her bed. She later described his face as looking 'thin and drawn'. The boy appeared to be in some distress, and was clawing at her arm. Mrs Herbert thought he was asking her to call his mother. When Mrs Herbert called 'Mummy', the boy disappeared.

The following evening Mrs Ross asked Margaret Minney if a little boy had ever died in the house. Miss Minney replied that her brother Johnny had, from meningitis. Before dying, he had been terribly ill, Miss Minney said, and had called for 'Mummy'.

This case was then investigated by G W Lambert, former Assistant Under Secretary of State for War, who was also interested in psychical research. He decided that there was no natural or ordinary explanation. Mrs Herbert, he said, had only just arrived at Waresley and would have had no opportunity to hear any village gossip about Johnny Minney. Furthermore, she had no idea that a little boy had ever died in the house. There was only one photograph of Johnny, aged three and this had never been seen by Mrs Ross as it was always kept in a drawer. Nor did Mrs Ross know that Miss Minney's brother had died in the house. Andrew MacKenzie sums up this case as one of 'retrocognition', in other words 'paranormal knowledge of past events beyond the range of inference or memory on the part of the subject'.

Sometimes inanimate objects may contain some hidden malevolent power. One such story is told by psychic investigator Philip Paul. A Mrs Dorothy Jenkins, who lived in Putney, south London, bought a large picture of a Victorian lady, signed 'Antoine', which she had seen in a junk shop. It hung in various parts of Mrs Jenkins' house for five years, when she said she could stand it no longer. The picture, she said when she called in Mr Paul to investigate, had brought her nothing but trouble, yet she was afraid to destroy or sell it.

Both Mrs Jenkins and her grown-up son, who lived with her, had suffered serious breakdowns since the picture entered the house, and Mrs Jenkins said that its eyes followed her around the room. Then the Jenkinses experienced serious financial difficulties that they felt certain were connected with the picture. When Mrs Jenkins' son, then in his thirties, sat down to dinner he heard voices telling him not to eat. As a result he had lost his appetite almost completely, and was thin and pale. His troubles had occurred since the picture had been moved from his mother's bedroom into his bedroom.

Philip Paul felt that the best way to investigate the picture was to get a recognized medium along to the house, so he contacted Ena Twigg, in those days the most famous medium in the country. When she arrived, Ena was blindfolded and told nothing of the events in the house. She moved round the room, placed her hands on the offending picture and instantly recoiled in horror, saying, 'There is great distress. There is a feeling of shaking all over.' Ena continued: 'I want to see Mum, that is the only person I feel safe with. A lot of lights. I can see blood. Soldiers of the Queen. They have injected the truth drug. They won't even let me shave myself properly.'

These remarks of Ena Twigg's accurately reflected the troubles experienced by Mrs Jenkins' son, who was not present at the time. Ena touched all the other pictures on the walls, but there was no reaction from any of them. After the session, Philip Paul advised Mrs Jenkins to get rid of the picture, which she did. Her troubles and those of her son ceased.

Philip Paul was also involved in investigating one of the most famous 'haunted houses' of this century – Borley Rectory, which burned down and was eventually demolished in the 1940s. The rectory attracted widespread media interest in 1940 when the book *The Most Haunted House in England*, written by famous psychic researcher Harry Price, appeared. According to Price, a huge number of paranormal phenomena had been witnessed at the rectory. They included many sightings of a phantom coach and horses; throwing of stones; whisperings and footsteps; strange odours; spontaneous outbreaks of fire; an organ playing in a locked and empty church nearby; and strange lights in windows.

The rectory had originally been built for the Reverend Henry Bull, who had fourteen children. A subsequent rector, Alfred Henning, who took over the living in 1936, felt he could not live there and Borley was put on the market. Because of its association with haunted happenings it was impossible to sell, and Harry Price himself lived there for a year, rent-free, to investigate the alleged ghosts.

Not long after Price's book was published, other reports began to appear saying that many of his apparitions had been faked and that he was not a reliable investigator. In 1954, by which time Harry Price had died, Philip Paul decided to try to get to the bottom of the Borley Rectory mystery himself.

He went to see the Reverend Bull's only surviving child, Ethel Bull, then in her eighties, who confirmed that she had seen the ghostly nun gliding towards her. The family cook had also sighted the 'nun' leaning over a gate, and for a time everyone was convinced that she was a real person. The Reverend Henning had witnessed a number of supernatural happenings around the rectory, and in 1948 had published his own account of the mystery. The Coopers, a couple who worked for the Bull family from 1916 to 1920, heard crashes in the kitchen. When they went to investigate, they found that nothing had been touched. One night Mr Cooper saw a black coach, drawn by a pair of horses, sweep into the rectory courtyard and then vanish. The Reverend Bull possessed no such vehicle.

A ghostly apparition was also sighted by Dr Margaret Abernethy, a local GP, in August 1949, when the rectory was no longer in existence. She was out in her car making house calls when she noticed a nun stooping amongst the weeds where the rectory garden had been. Dr Abernethy told Philip Paul that the figure seemed to be about forty, and absolutely normal in every respect. Dr Abernethy remembered that there was a convent about three miles away and decided to offer the nun a lift, as the weather was hot and oppressive. So she reversed into the gateway, only to find the nun had vanished. She made a quick search of the area, but soon realized there was no possible place for a nun, or anybody else for that matter, to hide. Dr Abernethy told Philip Paul: 'I don't care. I saw what I saw and there's an end of it'. Paul records in his book *Some Unseen Power* that a week or two later, when the grass was being cut, an old rosary was found deep in the grass.

Intrigued by all these accounts, Paul mounted his own investigation of Borley Rectory, accompanied by television crews from *Panorama*, including Richard Dimbleby, and newspaper men. He and his team made many excavations and discovered that Borley had been built over a far older building, dating back to the sixteenth century. A *Picture Post* photographer arrived and one of his pictures, later published in that magazine, showed what appeared to be a flying bird beyond the rectory gateway. There was much excitement at this picture, which was headlined: 'Is this the Borley ghost?' Philip Paul, himself a former newspaper journalist, says that the photographers and darkroom assistants assured him that nothing had been done to 'create' the mystery of the bird.

Paul ended his work at Borley after several leading mediums had come forward to say they had been in touch with the spirit of Harry Price, who told them the rectory and area round it was definitely haunted. But as with most ghost-hunting stories, no firm conclusion could be drawn from the evidence. Certainly no ghosts appeared when the Panorama team were filming, and Philip Paul himself never saw a ghost there.

One of the most famous 'ghost stories' of this century is that of the so-called 'Ghosts of Versailles' – eighteenth-century figures which were seen by two academics, Miss Annie Moberly and Miss Eleanor Jourdain, in the park of the Petit Trianon in August 1901. The two women published a book on their sightings and subsequent investigations, called *An Adventure*: it went out of print in 1955 owing to a decision made by Dame Joan Evans, then owner of the copyright, that the eighteenth-century figures supposedly seen by the two women were in fact real people – Count Robert de Montesquiou and some of his companions, in fancy dress, who were giving poetry readings.

In his book *Hauntings and Apparitions*, Andrew MacKenzie says that the eighteenth-century figures spotted by the two women have been seen by very many subsequent visitors to the place. The 'Ghosts of Versailles' have been subjected to an enormous amount of research, and the conclusion is that the sightings cannot just be dismissed. This case, says MacKenzie, is one of the strongest on record for the existence of supernatural beings. Miss Jourdain and Miss Moberly themselves exhaustively investigated the history behind the sightings, and came up with a possible, though still supernatural, explanation. After shifting through the evidence, MacKenzie comes to the conclusion that there simply is not a 'natural' explanation of the ghosts – they have been seen by too many people, and there is not a 'commonsense' explanation which fits.

Ghosts and other human apparitions have been explained by those who believe in them as earthbound spirits which have not been able to free themselves from the place where they died. They are usually associated with violent or untimely death, and are almost always young – those who have not lived out their allotted earthly time span. Ghosts are usually harmless, although frightening to those who sight them.

The trouble is that they nearly always melt away when sceptical researchers come to investigate them. Often, they go away at this point and never return, as with the Borley ghosts. Dr Ian Stevenson has said that 'when an investigator attempts to probe reports of spontaneous cases, a very considerable number of them simply melt away or prove worthless'. The Versailles ghosts are among the very few investigated which have not inconveniently disappeared.

## Out-of-the-body experiences

Surveys undertaken since the 1950s, when OOBEs first began to be seriously studied, suggest that around one in ten ordinary people will at some time in their lives undergo an out-of-the-body experience. This usually takes the form of having a very strong sensation of leaving the body and then observing it from some distance away. Sometimes, people having an OOBE believe they may have died without knowing it. Although they can be extremely frightening, OOBEs are not normally harmful in any way. People often wonder, when they are 'out of the body', whether they will ever be able to get back, but they always do.

In some ways, the OOBE is similar to a near-death experience: many people who have been near death and then returned speak of a sensation of floating above the body. However, one does not have to be near death for an OOBE to occur, although it is common during sleep, when resting, meditating, or feeling extremely relaxed – OOBEs often occur quite spontaneously, when the person is least expecting it.

In his book *The Reality of the Paranormal*. Professor Arthur Ellison describes a typical OOBE. People are often lying down, although not always, when they experience a strange feeling and seem to hear a sound like rushing wind or the sea. They then appear to float out of alignment with the body, so that they can observe the room from a different position and not through their physical eyes. But although the physical eyes are not being used, things can be seen. In fact, many sensations are apparent during an OOBE. The experience sometimes occurs during general anaesthesia, when the patient seems to be floating at the top of the operating theatre and watching the surgeons performing the operation. These OOBEs might be dismissed as fantasy, except that there are a number of instances on record where patients have been able to describe exactly what was going on as if from a position above the operating table. This does not of course in itself prove the reality of the OOBE, as the patient could have read up all about the operation beforehand.

It is common for those undergoing an OOBE to have a sensation that they are being pulled through the head; those who have experienced this say that it feels most unpleasant and is quite frightening. Others say that they seem to slip through their feet, while others float up horizontally. There are a number of ways in which people say they go 'out of the body', but whichever way the body is left the person always retains the ability to see and watch and hear what is going on.

But once the body has been left, the room that the person is in often changes. Things are seen which are not actually there. Windows may have bars on them, or there may appear to be bags and luggage in the room which are not in fact there. Sometimes there seems to be an unearthly kind of glow in the room, and the contents of the room (whether real or imagined) can always be seen quite clearly, even though it may be pitch black with no light on. Professor Ellison concludes from all this that what is being seen during an OOBE is not the room itself, but a dramatized reconstruction of a memory of the room. It is being seen only with the 'inward eye'.

Sometimes people undergoing an OOBE try to move an object or switch a light on. When they do this, they commonly find that their fingers go right through the light switch and nothing happens. They have become 'ghostly' entities with no substance – but during the OOBE they often cannot understand why this should be. Nor is the 'other' body clothed in its normal garments. It is common for OOBErs to report being dressed in flowing Grecian robes, or in something quite different from the real physical body down below.

Very often, says Professor Ellison, people undergoing OOBEs attain temporary clairvoyant powers. Ellison himself undertook an experiment to see if he could experience the sensation of being apparently separate from his physical body. He read all the books he could find on the subject and then, before going to sleep, spent an hour each night trying to will such an experience. One exercise supposed to induce an OOBE is to go to bed thirsty and then imagine going to the kitchen for a drink of water. Another recommended exercise involved imagining oneself looking at the ceiling while lying on one's back, and then letting the vision move across the ceiling – without actually moving the physical body at all.

About a month after practising these exercises, his experiences began. He found one night that he literally could not move a muscle. Then he attempted to float vertically upwards. The feeling, Professor Ellison says, was

> exactly as though I was embedded in the mud at the bottom of a river and the water was slowly reducing the viscosity. I gradually became free and began to float upwards. As though my eyes were now open, I observed the ceiling approach, I passed smoothly through it, noticing no obstruction, and entered the darkness of the space beneath the roof. I then floated freely through the tiles, my body still cataleptic and horizontal, and my speed gradually increased. I could see the moon and clouds quite clearly and to this day I remember the wind whistling through my hair as I shot rapidly up into the sky – horizontal, cataleptic and dressed in pyjamas!

On other occasions Professor Ellison was able to 'float' through the window, but one time when he was about to descend to the lawn of his garden he felt two hands holding his head. The hands moved him back into the room and downwards into his body. He says in his book that there are two possible explanations for this – either that discarnate entities were watching over him, or that his unconscious did not want him to go down to the lawn while out of the body. Ellison said that after experimenting with OOBEs for about a month he had to give it up, as it was making him tired and inefficient at work. He believes that out-of-the-body experiences prove that mind is non-material, distinct from body, and that information can be acquired while in this state of being 'separate'.

One of the best-known commentators on out-of-the-body experiences is Robert Monroe, a former businessman who founded a research institute in Virginia to monitor out-of-the-body experiences after undergoing several dramatic ones of his own. Several of these were quite alarming and included Monroe being struck by a beam out of the sky, seeing a ring of sparks circling his body like a hula-hoop, and gently bumping against the ceiling of his bedroom when 'out of the body'. When these experiences first occurred Monroe went to see doctors, but they could not offer any explanation of the phenomenon. So he decided to investigate for himself, undertake experiments, and see if he could get to the bottom of the mystery. He now operates a laboratory in which he produces out-of-the-body experiences for willing volunteers. These are Robert Monroe's hints on how to achieve an out-of-the-body experience.

You first have to be in a state of deep relaxation. Some subjects have had OOBEs while under the influence of a drug such as hash. Sensory deprivation, where you lie in a darkened room with no sound or interruption of any kind, is also often a precursor to the experience. Several American and Russian astronauts have described out-of-the-body experiences when they were being trained in sensory deprivation to prepare them for the space flights. The astronauts found themselves apparently floating in another body, sometimes high in the air. From their great height, they were able to see what was going on in the room clearly.

In India, meditation has been the traditional way to achieve an out-of-the-body experience. In his book *The Third Eye*, Lobsang Rampa claims that, in his Tibetan monastery, the lamas were taught to leave their bodies by intense meditation and experience 'astral travel'. This has also been claimed by several contemporary gurus, and advanced students of transcendental meditation claim to be able to levitate. But here, as with the ghost stories, it is notoriously difficult to prove that the person alleging the astral travel or levitation is actually telling the truth.

Although there has now been a considerable body of research into OOBEs nobody knows for sure what they really are. Are they a manifestation of some peculiarity of the brain – some fault in the electrical wiring, so to speak – or are they genuine indications that we possess some non-material entity which can survive separately from the body?

# Déjà vu

Nine out of ten people, according to surveys on the subject, will never experience an OOBE, but most of us have had the feeling of *déjà vu*, when we are certain we have been in a certain place before. Of course, very often we will have seen the place in a film, on television, or read about it in a book and then completely forgotten about it. But can this explain every single instance of the phenomenon?

Psychical researchers say that there are many instances on record of *déjà vu* taking place when there has been no possibility that the subject could have had advance knowledge in the ordinary way. Examples include going into a strange house in which to your certain knowledge you have never been before, and somehow knowing where everything is, and the history of the house. For some people, pieces of music evoke strong memories even when they could not possibly have heard the music before. Most of us have had the experience of meeting somebody for the first time and experiencing an instant rapport. What is the explanation of this, other than that we have met them in a previous incarnation?

Professor Arthur Ellison reckons that *déjà vu* is unlikely to have a 'paranormal' explanation. In his book *The Reality of the Paranormal* he describes the strongest possibility – that, without being consciously aware, people who experience having been there before have seen the place, or something very like it, in a film or book and have then forgotten about it. Neurologists, he says, know that certain perceptions may be stored as memories rather than actual perceptions, and the whole business is connected with processing information in the brain rather than a memory from a previous existence.

He does admit, though, that in some cases people may have had a precognitive dream of some kind, or gained the information in some other psychic or telepathic way. The fact that we do possess some kind of 'sixth sense' appears beyond dispute. It is not confined to humans, either: even more frequently animals pick up the 'vibrations' of a place or a person, and react accordingly.

For reincarnationists, *déjà vu* and ESP can easily be explained in terms of *karma* – the place or the person (in another body, of course) in some previous existence. For non-reincarnationists, ESP and *déjà vu* provide extremely weak or inadmissible evidence. There is probably a natural explanation for *déjà vu*, they say, especially these days when we all watch so much television and see so many films; and as for ESP, it most likely acts like radio or television waves, which, although we cannot see them, are nevertheless not supernatural. We can send out thought waves to people which are then picked up – it doesn't mean we have met them before, in another earthly existence.

## What does all this tell us?

In themselves, so-called paranormal phenomena are no proof or indication of any kind that we may be reborn into other bodies when we die. The most that open-minded and scrupulously conducted research into these areas can tell us is that there may well be something beyond the five senses, a non-physical aspect of humans which nevertheless has a strong reality of its own. This reality may be only tenuously connected with the body.

A century or so of scientifically conducted research into the paranormal has not really got us very far. At most, sceptics may grudgingly admit that there may be 'something' that we don't yet understand about the human mind and brain.

The question of whether ghosts exist, and whether they manifest themselves on occasion to susceptible people, has never really been solved, in spite of many exhaustive ghost hunts this century. Ghosts have a horrible habit of never turning up when you want them, and never providing the kind of information which would give conclusive proof of their existence. When I was working on a mass-selling Sunday tabloid we were always being sent to investigate claims that people could levitate, bend spoons, manifest ectoplasm or perform some other amazing example of paranormal phenomena. But without exception the ghosts and the ectoplasm failed to materialize when we turned up with our cameras. People who had allegedly levitated yesterday were mysteriously unable to do it today, when we were there to record the event. Those who had been paranormally bending spoons for months or even years failed every time to give us proof of their prowess when we were watching.

The usual explanation of this failure is that ghosts, levitators, ectoplasmic beings and so on 'know' when there is a sceptic in the room, and so fail to oblige. And, of course, the fact that ghosts are rarely seen whenever anybody sets out to investigate them doesn't mean they don't exist. It does, though, inevitably, put a big question mark over the whole subject of apparitions and 'sightings'.

Another problem with ghosts is that so many psychic investigators have themselves turned out to be fraudulent, or at the very least to have exaggerated their findings. Again, there is an understandable human reason for this. If you have spent months investigating a ghost and have poured large sums of money into the venture, you would naturally want to have some reward for your efforts. It's much more exciting to say you've seen a ghost than to report there was nothing there – there's no story in nothing. Moreover, nobody can say for absolute certainty that you haven't seen a ghost, because how can they provide absolute proof?

So for the time being I think we will have to put ghosts, earthbound spirits and other non-physical entities on to hold. They may exist, they may manifest, but as yet they must ultimately come into the category of whether you decide or not to believe in them – whether or not you feel that a belief in ghosts makes any kind of sense.

Poltergeists are different. Far too many people have witnessed poltergeist activity for us to be able to dismiss it as fantasy or rubbish. But because poltergeist activity always centres round teenagers and young people, and most often round those youngsters who are disturbed or living in bad family circumstances, I think it seems reasonable that there is a non-paranormal explanation for the phenomenon. Absolute sceptics say that the teenagers, or family in question, move the furniture around themselves and then allege it was a ghost. But although this may be the explanation in some of the cases, it doesn't fit them all. A number of reputable psychic investigators have witnessed for themselves frenetic poltergeist activity. The most likely explanation to me is that the objects are moved by some disturbed kind of energy emanating from the teenager.

One of the most famous poltergeist-type cases of recent times was the Amityville Horror, which was the subject of a couple of spine-chilling films. In 1974 Ronald DeFeo, aged twenty-two, shot and killed his mother, father, two sisters and brothers in the family's six-bedroomed house in Amityville on Long Island. Because of the murders the house was on the market for a very long time, and was eventually sold to the Lutz family for a very low price. The Lutzes consisted of George Lutz, aged twenty-eight, his wife Kathleen, thirty, and her three children from her first marriage.

Less than three months after moving into the house, the Lutzes reported strange and terrifying happenings. Demons, raps, slime, a black substance in the toilets, masses of flies, doors off their hinges, being touched by unseen presences – in fact, all the ingredients of a Gothic horror novel – terrified the Lutzes so much that they had to move. They wrote a book about their experiences and then moved to another house. The family experienced more paranormal terrors in their next two houses, but the next people to move to the Amityville house after the Lutzes found nothing untoward at all.

Near-death and out-of-the-body experiences cannot be so easily dismissed by even the most materialistic and mechanistic minds. Serious statistical and laboratory research on these two subjects has been carried out for almost two decades now, and to my mind provides the strongest evidence yet that we do possess something which is non-material, non-physical, which is not a part of matter but which nevertheless possesses some kind of consciousness. Of course, there are plenty of other possible theories – such as the effect of drugs, something going wrong with the wiring mechanism in the brain, or something going wrong with the whole works when we are near death. After all, we commonly experience a sensation of floating, of being outside the body, when we have a high fever or other serious illness.

The trouble is, the materialistic explanations do not begin to stand up for every single case. The fact that NDEs and OOBEs occur in all cultures, to all races, to people of every religious belief and none, to the educated and uneducated, and are pretty similar for everybody, points to at least the possibility that consciousness and memory are not part of the matter.

They don't give any kind of proof for reincarnation, of course, but they are a definite step on the way. There is simply no point in exploring even the idea of rebirth unless we accept the possibility that we possess a spirit of some kind. It is quite clear that nothing material of ourselves can reincarnate – so it must be the non-material aspect if anything.

People today, having got used to a century and a half of the scientific method, are not prepared to accept reincarnation, or the lack of it, on the basis of some kind of religious belief. Nor should they. We should only ever accept what makes sense, what adds up, what seems reasonable, after we have examined all the evidence that is available. After all, if rebirth exists, it exists, regardless of whether we believe in it or not – and vice versa.

The following chapter will sum up and evaluate the evidence for and against reincarnation that has been presented so far.

# CHAPTER SIX

# *The evidence for reincarnation*

## Religion and superstition

Most Westerners who dismiss the idea of reincarnation as superstitious non-sense do so without a minute's thought. But now, having assembled the available evidence on the subject, can we still dismiss it so easily?

As we have seen, throughout history most societies accepted rebirth as an absolute fact. This is not evidence, of course, but perhaps an indication that we should at least take the idea seriously. Although we cannot admit ancient beliefs as any kind of concrete proof, we must bear in mind that nobody has yet come along to prove beyond all possible doubt that there is no such thing as reincarnation.

Christianity, Islam and Judaism say there is no such thing as reincarnation; Hinduism and Buddhism state just as definitely that there is. But so far, religions have only been able to assert beliefs – none has offered any kind of evidence for their teachings on this subject.

## Memories of Ancient Egypt

So we have to look elsewhere for our evidence. A number of people, particularly in this century, have claimed that they have lived before; a few have written about the experience, and one or two have become famous because of it. But are the stories of Joan Grant, Dr Arthur Guirdham or Omm Sety any kind of evidence either?

Certainly they themselves believed fervently and absolutely in reincarnation, and all were intelligent, educated people. When Dr Denys Kelsey met Joan Grant in 1957 he was a Freudian psychiatrist working at Bart's Hospital, and had never given the subject of reincarnation any thought whatever. But he became convinced that Joan was genuine and, eventually, that rebirth was a fact of the human condition. He based much of his later work on this belief, and has had great success in treating patients with deep-seated phobias and neuroses. But, it has to be said, there is no way of proving beyond all possible doubt that Joan Grant really did live before. She may just have possessed an extremely vivid imagination.

The story of Omm Sety is perhaps a slightly stronger case. All her life, Dorothy Eady fervently believed that she had been Bentreshyt, a lowly girl who was the lover of a king. Her conviction took her to Egypt, where she lived for most of her life and she became a respected Egyptologist. But again her stories and experiences do not, I think, offer real proof of reincarnation because, intriguing though they are, it is simply impossible to prove beyond doubt that she was not making them up. There is just no known way of checking them out. Nobody can ever 'know' whether Joan Grant really was a winged Pharaoh, or a sixteenth-century strolling player; similarly, nobody can ever 'know' whether Dorothy Eady was in a previous incarnation the lover of an Egyptian king. We have to take their word for it – or not, as the case may be.

The group reincarnation experiences of Dr Arthur Guirdham, similarly, *could* have been fantasized. Although he comes up with plenty of evidence about himself and the others in his circle who were supposedly reincarnations of thirteenth-century Cathars, we have to take it all on trust. The stories of these three people give clues, and make us think, but there is nothing that would convince a dyed-in-the-wool sceptic.

## Hypnotic regression

So what about hypnotic regression, nowadays often considered a very strong indication of the reality of reincarnation? A growing number of avant-garde psychiatrists are now hypnotizing patients with chronic phobias and fears which do not seem to relate to any experience in this particular lifetime. The psychiatrists are claiming that, when they regress their patients back to a former life, they can very often trace the origin of the trauma and then bring it to the surface. After this, the patient is cured. Psychiatrists and hypnotherapists who use past-life therapy say that it is very successful and, often, the only kind of therapy which does work. But can we take their successes as proof of past lives?

I think not. Because again, as with the Joan Grant and Dorothy Eady stories, there is absolutely no method of checking out that the patient really has lived before. Even if documents and contemporary records are studied, and memories found to coincide, this still doesn't prove anything. The patient could have read a historical novel, seen a film, or remembered a history lesson from school. The 'memories' that come out under hypnosis cannot normally be accessed in any other way, and very often the patient has no recollection of the 'past life' that has been revealed while in a state of altered consciousness.

Researchers who have closely investigated 'past life' claims, such as Ian Wilson, have discovered that in every single case there is another interpretation to account for the memories. Most often, he says, the patients are exhibiting cryptomnesia – buried or forgotten memories which lie just beneath the surface and which have been forgotten by the conscious mind. It is usually these memories, rather than actual past lives, which come to the surface under hypnosis, he says. Wilson, who has certainly done his homework on following up 'regressed' subjects, may be right or he may be wrong. With present knowledge, there is simply no way of knowing for certain.

## Stand up and be counted

A more serious drawback, to my mind, with the cases of hypnotic regression, is that the psychiatrists and hypnotherapists are extremely coy about revealing the identities of their patients. In some cases this could be ascribed to preserving patient confidentiality, but I would have thought that patients who really have been helped to unearth their own past lives would not have wanted to keep quiet about it. When researching this book, I asked a number of doctors and hypnotists who had supposedly regressed people if they could put me in touch with some of their patients; all said they were unable to help. This meant that I could not check the stories out for myself. Also, when Ian Wilson went to see 'Jane Evans', who had unearthed at least six supposed past lives under hypnosis, she refused to talk to him. What did she have to hide? Wilson takes this as reasonably certain proof that she was making it all up.

The books by Dr Arthur Guirdham about the Cathars and group reincarnation, discussed in Chapter 3, seem at first to be pretty watertight. Here was a young woman patient who had persistent nightmares about terrible happenings during the thirteenth century, events she could not possibly have learned about at school, and which involved Arthur Guirdham himself as a member of the Cathar sect. When Dr Guirdham checked her story out – and he did this most meticulously, travelling to France and interviewing world experts on medieval French history – he discovered that his Mrs Smith was absolutely right in everything she had said and had written down in her notebooks as a teenager. Some commentators on the Guirdham story have said that if this is not a true example of reincarnation, we should have to find another explanation – and what other explanation could there be?

There could be another explanation, and that is that Dr Guirdham is making it all up. This explanation is at least as plausible as that a group of eight people, all living in the Bath area in the 1950s and 1960s, were actually members of a thirteenth-century heretical sect which was wiped out by the Inquisition. The very serious, major drawback to Dr Guirdham's books is that the main instigator of the whole story, Mrs Smith, remains anonymous. Why? What has she got to hide? Why hasn't *she* written the books, rather than Dr Guirdham? After all, she was the one with the nightmares, the one who could speak in fluent thirteenth-century French, the *langue d'oc*, which she could not have learned at school. Her story is far more exciting than that of Dr Guirdham, who, although he was supposed to have been Mrs Smith's lover in the thirteenth century, was really only on the periphery.

The same drawback applies to *Many Lives, Many Masters* by Brian Weiss, the latest addition to reincarnationist experiences. Why has he, and not 'Catherine', the patient, told the story? It would seem that, as a psychiatrist who is also a head of department, he would have far more to lose professionally than Catherine, who was described as a twenty-seven year-old lab assistant. And why does Catherine have to remain anonymous? Every single detail one could wish to know about Dr Weiss is included – his background, his marriage, his family, his career pattern. And yet he is not the interesting one – Catherine is. Why does her identity have to be so carefully protected?

The problem is that both Dr Guirdham's and Dr Weiss's stories are not copper-bottomed. The anonymity is a major stumbling block and there is no way of proving their stories beyond all doubt. They remain interesting reads, of course, but cannot give any kind of proof as to the reality of rebirth.

# Ian Stevenson's child subjects

So now we come to the many case histories collected by Dr Ian Stevenson. Here there are no neurotic female patients remembering past lives under hypnosis by a male therapist; here there is no anonymity, nothing to hide. In every single one of the cases collected by Dr Stevenson in which children remember previous lives, minute details are provided including their names, dates of birth, family background, names of family members, and a large amount of information about the supposed previous life. The children who remembered previous lives did so naturally and spontaneously; the information did not have to be dragged out of them when in a state of altered consciousness. And the children themselves were very ordinary girls and boys – not mentally disturbed, not neurotic, not particularly attention-seeking. They were, for the most part, extremely unremarkable ordinary children.

Dr Stevenson's researches have been carried out in the most meticulous way, all over the world. He says himself that they do not offer conclusive proof of reincarnation, but they are often difficult to explain in any other way.

Even so, sceptics have not been convinced. His detractors say that the children who supposedly remember previous lives very often recall an earlier existence in a far richer and more powerful family: there are few cases where the previous incarnation was further down the social or financial ladder. Also, detractors point out, Dr Stevenson was frequently having to rely on an interpreter – particularly when he was interviewing children from Indian or Malaysian villages, for example – and could not know whether the interpreter's translation was accurate. A further drawback to acceptance of Dr Stevenson's cases, say some, is that most of their subjects are from countries whose inhabitants believe in reincarnation anyway, and would not have to be convinced. The child would hear talk of previous lives as naturally as, in Western families, television programmes would be discussed.

Many of Stevenson's case histories are difficult to pick holes in; but even so, I do not think they would offer proof to the determined sceptic. For those who already believe in reincarnation, Dr Stevenson's work does seem to offer conclusive proof – but not to those who do not. They say the children could have made up the stories; they could have heard their parents talking about them; or they could have picked up the information about their supposed previous life in a number of non-supernatural ways. The cases, numerous though they are, do not offer irrefutable evidence of rebirth to the total unbeliever.

## Ghosts and other aspects of the paranormal

So what about ghosts, NDE's, OOBEs and other manifestations of the paranormal? I think ghosts and apparitions can be dismissed, at least as evidence of some kind of survival after death. Those who believe in spirits and the spirit world explain ghosts and apparitions by saying that they are earthbound spirits who have not managed to transport themselves to the astral spheres.

The problem with ghosts, though, is that they never seem to manifest themselves when their presence is most wanted, such as when investigators or television crews are in the vicinity. Surely, if ghosts existed and did have some kind of external reality, they would be able to be seen by large numbers of people, instead of a very few? It is perfectly possible that 'ghosts' and other apparitions simply exist in the minds and consciousness of gullible or suggestible people. Those who don't believe in ghosts hardly ever seem to see them, and it's just not good enough to attempt to explain this by saying that they just disappear and dematerialize whenever they can sense an unbeliever around. If there are such things as ghosts, and if there are such things as earthbound spirits, they will have to do something more dramatic then they have hitherto managed to convince sceptics of their reality.

Another disincentive to belief is that the whole subject is so shrouded in fakery and fraud. Although there may be such a thing as genuine ghosts, there is not yet, to my mind, strong enough evidence for their existence. In more than a hundred years of investigations into the subject, the various societies for physical research have not come up with a shred of convincing evidence that ghosts and apparitions are a reality.

The world of mediums, channels and sensitives similarly offers extremely flimsy 'evidence' of survival after death. We can never know for certain that they really are in touch with discarnate entities. Even when the medium displays knowledge that could not easily have been obtained by ordinary means, it still offers no proof whatever that there are discarnate entities existing somewhere in the starry spheres, ready to dispense wisdom through specially chosen people. There are so many unanswered questions about mediums and channels. Why is it that these entities only come through certain people? Why aren't we all in touch with them? Why are they so elusive about themselves? So far, the whole thing is just not good enough.

An exception probably has to be made for the work of Edgar Cayce: there seems little doubt that he was absolutely genuine and did not stoop to any kind of fraud. But we cannot take even this amazing example as concrete evidence that we all lived before and shall be born again. Most of us cannot go to sleep and then receive incredible amounts of knowledge, or be able to heal sick people from vast distances. Edgar Cayce remains an unexplained phenomenon, but one single example of a genuine paranormal healer could not convince an unbeliever about life after death.

The near-death experience, which has now been extensively scientific-ally studied in a number of universities and hospitals all over the world, offers the best evidence yet that there is some kind of survival after death. But at the very best, the NDE only demonstrates that we can survive the first intimations of death. Nobody has ever come back from real death to tell us what it is like on the 'other side'. It could be that the light at the end of the tunnel, the sensations of bliss and peace, only accompany near death – not actual death – and that there is nothing whatever beyond the grave or the crematorium.

It does not seem likely, from the research undertaken so far, that the NDE can be explained away by biochemists or neurologists. The very similar out-of-the-body experience, though, could be caused by some temporary wrong wiring of neural connections in the brain. To me, the evidence of survival offered by OOBEs is not nearly so strong as that amassed from the study of NDEs.

The point is that very, very few of us have ever seen a ghost, have ever had an NDE or an OOBE, have any memory whatever of a previous life or are able to communicate with discarnate entities. Until these experiences become more common, most of us will continue to regard anything to do with the paranormal or supernatural with a very large pinch of salt. So far, there is simply no good scientific evidence which proves beyond a shadow of a doubt that we all reincarnate many, many times and that we possess a soul or spirit which is immortal and can never die, whatever we might do.

## The only logical answer to life?

So does this mean there are no good reasons for believing in reincarnation? No. I think that there is plenty of good evidence, but that we have to look for another kind of satisfying explanation.

I think we have to ask ourselves whether a belief in reincarnation makes any kind of sense, whether it appeals to irrefutable logic, whether it is likely to improve the quality of life, and whether it is likely to alter our perceptions and attitudes for the better or not. If a belief in reincarnation makes sense of the otherwise senseless and inexplicable, then we may consider we are getting somewhere.

To my mind, the very best evidence for the existence of reincarnation is that it explains the otherwise completely inexplicable. It offers a very good reason why there is so much apparent injustice and unfairness in the world, and enables us to make sense out of life, and what happens to us. Those who do not believe in reincarnation and *karma* – and, of course, the two concepts are inextricably intertwined – offer no satisfactory explanation as to why some people are born with every privilege and others experience nothing but deprivation and misery. Why, for example, are some children born handicapped? If you are a non-reincarnationist, you can't even begin to say why this might be.

Of course, we can say that handicaps result from a defective gene, from the mother smoking or drinking during pregnancy, perhaps, or from brain damage suffered at birth. But while all this may tell us *how*, it doesn't begin to explain *why*. As we all know, we are by no means born equal. Within the same family some of the children may be bright, beautiful and talented, while other children may be dim, plain and unlikeable. A recent novel by Doris Lessing, *The Fifth Child*, is the story of a child born to a particular family who was completely unlike all the others – a difficult, devilish child. This novel questions why, with exactly the same genetic mix, one child should be horrible, while the rest of the children are decent human beings?

Science, medicine and psychology can only offer theories – they cannot give any reasons. If we accept that rebirth and *karma* might be a fact of the human condition, all these things become immediately more explicable. There is no possible good reason why one child should be born handicapped, in poverty, or to suffer at the hands of adults – unless something has happened in the past to make this suffering an inevitable consequence of what has gone before.

People often ask how it is that a God who is supposed to be all-wise, all-loving, all-benevolent, can let terrible things happen in the world. How, they ask, can a God who is supposed to be fundamentally good let innocent people starve or be tortured to death? How could He have let six million Jews, many of them children, be exterminated in concentration camps? The Jews had done nothing to deserve this terrible fate.

For a non-reincarnationist, there is no answer to this. The religious person, Christian, Jew or Muslim, might say that the reward for earthly suffering is a place in Heaven. But this is all superstition, and cannot really appeal to the logical, rational mind. We have no guarantee, no evidence, that Heaven exists, or that the good go to Heaven and the bad go to Hell. In any case, who decides what is good or bad? Few people are completely criminal or utterly saintly.

The Catholics have an answer for earthly wrongs – you have to spend a time in purgatory, so that you can earn your place in Heaven. But again, whether purgatory exists or not can only be a matter of speculation. None of us knows, and in any case the existence of purgatory does not begin to make up for injustice on earth.

But if we acknowledge the possibility that we have earned our place in the world, our level of health and happiness, by what we did in previous lives, that what we are experiencing now is the direct consequence of what we have done in the past, then everything starts to make more sense. Instead of wailing: why me? (to which there is no good answer) we can be sure that we have brought about our present circumstances by our past actions. In a very real way, we are reaping what we have sown.

In the Bible it says: cast thy bread upon the waters and it shall come back to you after many years. It may seem unfair that we have to wait for another birth to even things up, but it is unarguable that injustices and unfairnesses are not always sorted out in this life. It is evident that criminals often get away with murder, literally, and never have to atone for their bad deeds. If they are psychopaths, they don't even have any remorse about what they have done, so their conscience doesn't trouble them.

The Reverend Dr Leslie Weatherhead, a famous Methodist minister, came to believe that reincarnation provided the only logical answer to life. As he says in his booklet *A Case for Reincarnation*, first published in 1958, there is no proof and there is never likely to be – not of a scientific kind, anyway. Dr Weatherhead refers to passages in the Bible which talk of reincarnation, where Jesus Christ accepted reincarnation as a fact. Speaking of John the Baptist in Matthew 11, he says: 'This is Elijah which is to come.'

If, as Christians, we believe that God is just, we more or less have to believe in reincarnation, he feels; otherwise life is completely unfair. Dr Weatherhead gives two examples to illustrate just how unfair life can apparently be. On the one hand, he says, there is Betty Smith, born into a prosperous home, given a good education, marrying a loving man, keeping in good health, having a number of happy, healthy children, and surviving into content old age. On the other hand there is Jane Jones, born blind or deaf or crippled into a poverty-stricken home with a drunken father who makes her life a misery. Jane dies an early death of malignant disease.

Where is the justice here? It is no answer, says Dr Weatherhead, to say that everything will be squared up in Heaven. Because although Jane Jones may experience heavenly bliss, is this to be denied to Betty Smith because she has enjoyed her earthly life? Punishing Betty in Heaven for Jane's unhappiness on earth would make no sense at all. And anyway, what kind of heavenly compensation makes up for utter misery on earth? The two states are not similar in any way. And what about a man who has been imprisoned, or even put to death, for a crime he has not committed? How will anybody ever make it up to him?

So, Dr Weatherhead asks, is human distress just a matter of the luck of the draw? Is it pure chance whether we draw the short straw or the long straw of life? Are health and happiness, wealth and contentment, simply a matter of chance and coincidence? If so, he says, 'how unlike any human father He must be, for a human father who thus exerted his will would be clapped in jail.' He goes on:

But if we accept the idea that all these inequalities are the result
– in a cosmos of cause and effect – of earlier causes, the
product of some distant past, the fruit of earlier choices, then our
sense of justice is preserved. The mangled body then is not a
greater mystery than the mangled body at the foot of a cliff,
mangled because its owner did not look where he was going.

If we only have the one earthly life, argues Dr Weatherhead, nothing is satisfactorily answered. There is no possible explanation of why some children are born with inherent talents while other children, perhaps in the same family, are not. Musical children do often, it is true, come from musical families, but by no means always, and in any case, very great talent has often emerged completely out of the blue. Where has it come from?

Geneticists may believe that it is all in the genes, but cannot explain why the genetic mix should appear so absolutely random and chancy. As biologists know, nothing else in nature is completely random, but conforms to set laws.

Religious people may say that terrible handicap or mutilation is some kind of punishment from God. But again, this doesn't really make any kind of sense. Why should a supposedly innocent child, just born, have to suffer a handicap? And why should the child's parents have to suffer by bringing up such a child, or watching it die?

But if we can accept the possibility that we have somehow brought our present conditions upon ourselves, we can begin to understand why they might have happened. It is not God, but ourselves who are responsible for ourselves. The terrible scourge of AIDS is, to a non-reincarnationist, completely inexplicable. Why should these people, who have often done no harm other than have an active sex life, have succumbed to this dreadful and fatal disease? Is God punishing them for being promiscuous? Most researchers into AIDs reject the 'God's punishment' theory out of hand. Why should black people, homosexuals, drug addicts, be singled out for particular punishment by God? But if we accept that it is the past *karma* of these people which has brought about their present affliction, then we can begin to understand it.'

If we see all ill health, all inequalities, all injustice, as the result of *karma*, we can not only begin to interpret life much more meaningfully; we can also do something about it. We can make up our minds not to engage in any action which will inevitably have a bad result. A belief in reincarnation teaches us that we can never escape the consequences of our own actions. This means that if we do good actions, good will result – and vice versa. Whatever we do creates an inevitable ripple. We may not know the full extent of the consequences of any action, but we can be sure that there is no action without an equal and opposite reaction. It is a law of nature – why should humans be exempt from it?

The reincarnationist idea makes sense of otherwise completely inexplicable events such as the Holocaust, famine, wars, the dropping of atom bombs and so on. The reason that six million Jews were murdered in concentration camps is that these people had somehow done something to deserve this fate in a previous life. It was their *karma* to perish – not that this in any way excuses the action of the Nazis, of course, because by their deeds they will have set even more terrible things in motion for the future.


## An alternative approach to death

Once the possibility of reincarnation is accepted, then death has a very different meaning. There has been much talk lately about the rights and wrongs of abortion. More than twenty years after the Abortion Law Reform Act came into force in Britain, there are still people who are trying to outlaw the act. Many of these are Christians, a large proportion of whom are Catholics who believe that any killing must be wrong. But seen through the reincarnationist perspective, abortion takes on a new and different meaning.

If we accept that humans possess a soul and that this soul is immortal, then we understand that it cannot be killed. If a foetus is killed before it has a viable life, then the soul will simply pass out of that body and into another one. It is the *karma* of the incoming soul to live in a particular body for a very short time. This does not mean, of course, that it is all right to kill because the souls, once released, will simply find another body to inhabit; it is not all right to kill, because the consequences of that murder will rebound on to the murderer. But, to a reincarnationist, it is impossible to kill a person; you can only destroy the body, the very temporary housing of that soul.

Once we accept the idea of reincarnation, physical death becomes far less frightening and final. A belief in rebirth allows us to understand that we never die, but simply shed this physical overcoat once it can no longer serve us well. If more people believed in reincarnation, the present ghoulish business of organ transplantation, of keeping people artificially alive far beyond the body's own natural capabilities, would cease.

The belief also makes sense of the idea of the immortality of the soul. Christians believe that the soul comes into existence at conception, or at some stage before birth, and from then on is immortal. But surely, the word 'immortal' means no beginning and no end? If a soul *begins* life at some point, then it is by definition finite.

# The possibility of leading better lives

The great advantage of a belief in reincarnation is that it enables us to become better people, to be far more careful of our relationships, our actions, the way we live our lives. It allows us to take full responsibility for ourselves and not to blame others. We are what we are because of past *karma*, not because our mothers smoked, our fathers were violent, or whatever. The belief also allows us to alter our circumstances for the better, to accept that we can improve our present condition and do not have to languish in agony because of what our parents or relatives or early circumstances have done. All reincarnationist philosophies teach that it is possible to reverse bad *karma*, to bring about positive changes by deciding to live a better life and so not attracting more bad *karma* to ourselves.

Once we believe in reincarnation, we are far less likely to be malicious, deceitful, criminal, dishonest – because we understand that everything bad we do will rebound back upon ourselves, inevitably. Our reward or otherwise will not be in Heaven, but here on earth, in some future life.

# Changing relationships

If the soul is immortal, and has lived many times before, then of course nobody is 'innocent'. A child is not a child, but a soul who at the moment inhabits a small body. That child's soul may be as old as, or older than, yours. Also, it is very possible that children born into particular families at this time were also family members in a past life. Those who have delved into their own past lives commonly find that the people they are associating with now were also important to them in past bodily existences.

When we consider the possibility of reincarnation, we instantly become less attached to members of our own families, and to marriage or other intimate partners. We should not be sad when marriages break up, or when the love and regard which were once present have died away. If we interpret changing relationships as *karma* working itself out, then we will be more content to let people go and to carry on without them. We will not want to bind people to ourselves perpetually against their will. We will take responsibility for ourselves, but not for other people.

Of course, we have to be responsible for children and other dependants if they are incapable of looking after themselves. But once children have become independent we should be able to let them live their own lives. For they are not 'our' children. All we have done, as parents, is to enable their souls to inhabit a body. We have provided the body – but we have not provided the soul, nor are we responsible for their personality, talents and behaviour in this life. These are the aspects they have brought with them and which we can do precious little to alter. If a child has amazing musical talent, we as parents can encourage this or we can try to stifle it. But the fact that this talent is possessed is not due to our own cleverness or good judgement.

In America at the moment there is a movement to try to create super-intelligent people by collecting the sperm of geniuses; some women have already given birth to babies in this way. But, although one may be able to cut down the odds of having a congenital idiot or an unintelligent child by this means, one can never guarantee it. William, the one surviving child of the poet Shelley and his wife, – both geniuses – grew into a completely ordinary man who never wrote a line of poetry or uttered a memorable comment. The son of Elizabeth Barrett Browning and Robert Browning, also fairly evenly matched for genius, was not a genius himself. Children of famous, gifted, intelligent parents have often been extremely ordinary, while genius has been born in the most unpromising circumstances. It is obvious that a child does not start life with a clean slate on which is then written successive experiences. Nurses in maternity hospitals observe that babies start to exhibit distinctive characteristics almost as soon as they are born: one will be content, another fractious.

## How does reincarnation work?

Assuming for the moment that reincarnation is a possibility, how does it all work? Why don't more of us remember past lives – and in any case, what exactly is it that reincarnates? So far, the only answer to that comes from religious beliefs – it is the mind, intellect and tendencies, or established habits, which continue indefinitely, and most of us don't remember because physical death acts as a kind of conscious wiping out. The effects of our past actions are there, but we may not consciously remember them. There are, so far, no scientific pointers to tell us just what continues, and what ends, at physical death.

Dr Ian Stevenson feels that reincarnation of some kind offers the best explanation of his many case studies. But the memories of those cases investigated are not ordinary ones. Almost all of the previous people have died violent or untimely deaths, usually both. They are people who have not completed what is considered a normal lifespan.

The abiding problem with the subject, he says, is that it cannot be studied scientifically and there is no real proof available one way or the other. In the end, it comes down to what makes most sense. For Dr Stevenson, there are no major difficulties in acknowledging the possibility of reincarnation. His view, after studying over two thousand cases, is that the entity which survives physical death is the mind and personality, both of which may undergo major modifications in the new body. In the cases he has investigated, although memories may be there, often the new personality is quite different.

The idea of reincarnation, says Stevenson, offers a valuable contribution to the uniqueness of individuals, and helps to explain why we are all so very different. The only people who have personality characteristics in common are identical twins who, in reincarnation theory, would be two beings whose *karma* is so similar that in this birth they have been born together and look alike as well. Most reincarnationists accept that each individual has his or her own soul, and that it is this which provides the 'life force' or energy to enable us to carry on living in a physical body.

It certainly may explain unusual behaviour on the part of some people. Certain people are often observed to behave in ways that bear no relation to their upbringing or circumstances, One very famous example is Florence Nightingale, who was brought up to be a lady of absolute leisure. Neither of her parents worked, and spent most of their time travelling and entertaining. Where did Florence get the idea to do something useful with her life? Certainly not from her social circle, to whom the idea of a woman working, let alone in such a lowly profession as nursing, was unthinkable.

Another very famous example is the composer Handel. There were no known musicians in his family, and his parents strenuously opposed his following a musical career. If unusual aptitudes and abilities do not appear because of previous lives, where do they come from? Genetics has no answers. Dr Stevenson points out, though, that no child prodigy has ever attributed his or her precocity to a previous life.

A previous life may also explain much illness and phobia, and many other medical and biological phenomena. Very many children have phobias which seem to bear no relation to any experience in this life.

Addictions and cravings, which are also often inexplicable, may be the result of events in previous lives. The phenomenon of transsexualism, which continues to baffle science and medicine, can be explained in terms of reincarnation. In his researches, Dr Stevenson has come across many children who simply do not fit into their gender role: when they remember a previous life, it was in the other gender. In this lifetime they are unable to adjust, and lead miserable lives unless they can be helped to make a cosmetic change and live as a member of the preferred sex. There is no psychiatry or behavioural technique available which will make it possible for true transsexuals to live happily in their original anatomical sex. They feel that it is all wrong, and that they have simply been given the wrong body. Although they may accept rationally that this is nonsense, nothing ever stops them from wanting to change over.

Ian Stevenson believes that reincarnation does not discredit the sciences of genetics, evolution and biology, but rather helps to explain them all. At the moment, no science offers any explanation of why humans should be so very different, or why there is often so much variety within the one family. The idea that genetic and behavioural differences come about through pure chance gives no clue to explaining the many inequalities in life, Stevenson says.

In *Children Who Remember Previous Lives*, he offers his opinions of the various types of 'evidence' that have been advanced in an attempt to prove reincarnation. He considers that the very weakest evidence comes from those who claim to be able to read other people's previous lives, either by talking to them or putting them under hypnosis. So often, says Stevenson, the previous lives remembered take place in well-known times or during dramatic events – the Crusades, the French Revolution, the extermination of the Cathars by burning at the stake, dynastic Egypt, major wars. By contrast, all the memories of the children interviewed by him are of very ordinary events. Even though in many cases the previous person died a violent or early death, the circumstances were still unremarkable, undramatic, unlikely to be recorded in history.

Another factor which discredits the past-life reading 'evidence', according to Stevenson, is that so often people only seem to remember one past life. If reincarnation is a reality, we must all incarnate many times.

Also, if Ian Stevenson's cases have any validity, they show us that reincarnation takes place almost instantaneously after death. This finding accords with the belief of the Brahma Kumaris, who teach that rebirth happens almost at once: there will be an interval of less than a year before the soul incarnates again. But so many claimed past lives were centuries and centuries ago.

In the case of Arthur Guirdham and the Cathars, what were they all doing between the thirteenth century and now? Did all this group who were burned at the stake or otherwise killed wait seven centuries to be reincarnated together as extremely unremarkable people in Bath?

Stevenson considers that hypnotic regression does not offer any real evidence of reincarnation, either. It would be all too easy for the hypnotist to make suggestions, or for the hypnotist and patient to collude in the 'past life' memory. After all, there are usually only the two people present at the session. There has grown up, Stevenson remarks, an idea that hypnotic regression offers the strongest evidence yet produced for reincarnation. But it is all too easy for fantasies to masquerade as memories. Nor is it possible to check out the stories objectively. If the claimed past life was a famous one, then there will be records which can be checked, but it doesn't prove anything. If the life was an obscure one in the past, then there will probably not be any records – and so nobody can check one way or the other. Either way, no proof is offered or obtainable.

So what about those hypnotists who claim to have cured people of long-standing phobias of water or flying, for example? Dr Stevenson's answer here is that the cure most probably lies with the skill of the therapist, rather then dragging up a supposed past life. But the 'past life' interpretation makes it all much more exotic and exciting.

Stevenson concedes that the children he has interviewed do often exhibit a phobia directly related to the manner in which they died, but there are, he says, no grounds for believing that recovering a past memory helps to abolish a phobia. In the cases investigated by Stevenson, the phobia remained even when the child was allowed to talk freely about the previous life. To Dr Stevenson, one very strong indication of the reality of a past life is the faculty of zenoglossy, in which people can speak in languages they have not learned in this lifetime and ordinarily do not know. There are several well-documented examples of zenoglossy on record.

*Déjà vu*, Stevenson believes, does not offer strong evidence. Although around 70 per cent of people report at least one incidence of it, there could easily be other explanations, such as having seen something similar, having read a book or watched a film. Dreams and nightmares could, he says, be leftovers from previous lives – but again, there can never be any real proof of this.

One big question is: why don't we all remember a previous life? It seems quite rare, even among those people who accept reincarnation without question. There are several answers. It could be that the Brahma Kumaris are right, and not everybody has had a previous life – that there are always new souls coming down to incarnate for the first time. Then again, it could be that we have had previous lives without remembering them at all. The fact that we don't remember anything about a past life does not necessarily mean we haven't had one – perhaps it was not very memorable or exciting, and so we have just forgotten about it. There is some evidence from ancient religions that in fact we are not supposed to remember previous lives, that our birth is 'but a sleep and a forgetting', as Wordsworth wrote. Ian Stevenson's researches showed that past lives were only remembered when they had ended suddenly, incompletely. This, he says, may have generated a craving for a very quick rebirth.

In addition, Ian Stevenson says that from his own researches it does not seem to be beneficial to this life, on the whole, to be able to remember a past one. Many children who recalled previous existences suffered – often from the attitude of their parents who simply did not understand what they were talking about. In any case, their memories were never happy ones – the children remembered illness, crimes, murder, sadness, but never pleasant happenings.

## Making a personal judgement

Ian Stevenson knows that his own researches will never convince those who demand proof and replication under laboratory conditions. He says that most of us suffer from neoideophobia, or fear of new ideas, and the idea of reincarnation is still unfamiliar enough in the West for many scientists and doctors to reject it out of hand. The fact that so many of his case histories have come from the Far East also adds to their unreliability in the eyes of scientists. We have great difficulties, he says, in separating the idea of the physical from the non-physical. We can accept the idea of growing older readily, but find it hard to take the concept of growing younger, or starting again.

Reincarnation, says Stevenson, is above all a doctrine of hope. It offers a positive, logical explanation of why things are as they are in the world, and why there is so much injustice and inequality. But it can be a hard doctrine to accept as it makes us take responsibility for our actions – it is no longer 'their' fault if things are unequal, unfair, miserable. If we acknowledge the idea of reincarnation, we have to accept that the reason we are like we are is because of what we have done in the past, and that it is not the fault of our parents or circumstances. We are born into a particular family, say reincarnationists, because somewhere along the line we have made karmic connections which need to be sorted out and finished. When people feel, as they often do, that they have no particular rapport with their families, this probably means that the karmic connections have now been severed, and the business, whatever it is, is finished. Dr Stevenson believes that, at the moment, we know almost nothing about reincarnation. We have to rely on assertions from religious organizations which teach rebirth, but we have no real evidence and no proof of any kind that we are reborn into new bodies when we die. At the end of the day, it's all a matter of whether a reincarnationist interpretation of the meaning of life appeals to your innate logic and sense of justice – or not.

# CONCLUSION

Like most people brought up in the Western Christian tradition, I grew up firmly believing that reincarnation was an archaic superstition. When, later, I decided I could no longer believe in Christianity, I still held on to the anti-reincarnationist teachings with which I had been indoctrinated in my youth. Now, though, I believe just as firmly that reincarnation must happen and that, indeed, to accept the concept is the only way of making any sense of life on earth.

So how have I come to change my views so radically? Simply by investigating the subject as thoroughly as I have been able to do, and listening to what those who do believe have to say on the matter.

Before embarking on my research for this book, I would have maintained that I had a completely open mind on the concept of rebirth. But actually, I now realize, I hadn't at all. Deep down, I still secretly considered those who believed in reincarnation to be either extremely gullible and simple-minded, or fantasists – trying to believe something which patently did not and could not be the case.

But when I began to look into the teachings more thoroughly, I learned that for many people reincarnation is not just a vague idea but a well worked out and completely logical philosophy of life – and death. Moreover, it has never been disproved. Those who hold that there is no such thing are simply making assertions – they cannot come up with a shred of evidence to support their belief.

You may say that those who believe in reincarnation have no evidence either. I agree that there is no conclusive proof available, and it seems as if there is never likely to be. But the point is that once you believe in reincarnation you can have a philosophy of life which answers many otherwise unanswerable questions. If not, you have no good explanation of why things are so monstrously unfair, why people are born into such widely differing circumstances, and why the guilty and the bad are very often not punished while the good seem to suffer.

Before confronting myself with reincarnationist teachings, I accepted that life was a meaningless jumble, a jungle where you tried to grab for yourself the best that your ability and personality permitted. I could see that life was lucky for some, horrendously unlucky for others, but supposed that this was how things were. I somehow accepted that we were not born equal, that this was the way of the world, and that things would never even up.

I could not as an adult believe in the Christian God because, contrary to what I had been taught in Sunday school, he did not appear to be merciful, nor did He ever intervene or answer prayers. God never seemed to lift a finger to help anybody, so far as I could see. He never averted tragedies, never stopped people being raped or murdered, never made ill people better. He never brought a shred of happiness to anybody, or alleviated sorrow. In fact the Christian God was pretty useless, it seemed. Although we were taught that Christ had come to save us, He too seemed singularly inept at saving anybody. And when, in history lessons, I came to learn the terrible things that had been done in the name of religion, there was no way I could believe in such a God.

If ever I asked myself why it was that children in the same family, for instance, were often born with widely differing personalities and abilities, I expect I thought that the answer lay in a complicated combination of genetic inheritance and environment. I remember a number of studies being carried out in the 1970s which tried to formulate a child's personality from his or her position in the family. The eldest child had such and such a personality, the middle one would be a different type of person, and the youngest one different again.

But although these investigations might shed a small amount of light on the question, they could not offer anything like a complete and satisfactory answer. For there were always many exceptions. The eldest child was not always the brightest and most confident, the middle one did not always conform to the 'middle' personality, and so on.

I now believe the answer to why children are so very different from each other, even when they have the same parents and a similar upbringing, will never be found by a study of genetics. But even if genetics could somehow explain how it all happened, it would not tell us *why* people were born into such differing circumstances, *why* one child had every privilege and happiness, while another, through apparently no fault of its own, knew only sorrow and suffering. No geneticist can ever tell us why, in the scheme of things, some children may be born handicapped, unhappy or with unlike-able personalities.

But the doctrine of reincarnation can explain all these things. It not only tells us how, but why – it answers the most important questions about human existence. To me it provides the master picture which enables us to complete the jigsaw, to fit all the pieces together.

I now strongly believe that most, if not all of us, have lived many, many times before and that it is these previous incarnations which account for both our present circumstances and our personalities. Obviously, in each life genetics and environment will play a part, but they will at most only interact with what is already there.

Having looked at all the possibilities, I have now formulated a set of beliefs which work for me. I don't know whether they are correct, as I have no possible means of verifying them. But they have the appeal of logic, and provide answers to the most profound questions about human existence.

Although I believe that we all incarnate many times, possibly infinitely, I don't and can't believe that we ever incarnate as animals or plants, or that such incarnations are 'punishments' for having lived a vicious or unsatis-factory life as a human. No one in this book has ever remembered a previous life as an animal. In any case, an incarnation as an animal would be pointless for a human. What lessons could we learn? How would we ever be 'good' enough as animals to merit reincarnation as a human at some future time?

Although it seems possible that animals, as well as humans, may have souls or spirits – animal owners will tell you that each of their pets or live-stock has a slightly different character – they patently do not engage in the kind of actions and interactions which characterize human existence. Animals do not fall in love, they do not kill each other except for food or self-preservation, they do not have the power of reflective thought, or the ability to change their environment. They do not progress with each incarnation.

It does seem likely, however, that human souls or spirits are neuter, and that we interchange between the sexes. I don't believe, as some ancient religions did, that incarnation as a woman is a punishment for not being a very satisfactory man, or that women are lower down the evolutionary scale. But just by simple observation we can see that all human characteristics can be found in either sex. There are aggressive women and passive men; intelligent women and stupid men; men who like looking after people, and men who are content to take orders rather than to give them – and vice versa for all of these. There are, in other words, 'feminine' men and 'masculine' women. No personality trait is seen only in one particular sex.

Of course social conditioning, hormones, environment, expectations and so on determine that men and women may lead very different lives. But there is not a specifically 'male' personality or a specifically 'female' one. I find now that it helps to regard people not as men or women, but as neuter souls temporarily inhabiting a male or a female body.

For a long time it was not easy for me to accept the idea that humans may have an eternal soul. Although this is what is taught in Christianity – and, indeed, all religions – I had firmly rejected this belief when I became an atheist. To me, the Christian teachings about the human soul seemed so much nonsense. Whenever I asked clergymen whether non-Christians would go to Heaven, they usually replied that it would only happen if they were saved by Jesus. The implication was that all non-Christians – the majority of people in the world – could not go to Heaven. But apart from that, there did not seem much point in having an eternal soul if we were just going to spend endless time adoring God, or, conversely, existing for ever in Hell, the place without God. So I decided, along with other atheists, that humans did not have a soul, that the personality died along with the body.

But once I accepted the possibility of reincarnation, the idea that we have an eternal soul, or non-physical component, began to have a point. I now believe that all humans must have this element, and that it incarnates into new bodies all the time. The type of body and set of circumstances in which we find ourselves is a direct consequence of what has gone before. We may never know what has led us into our present circumstances, but I think now that we can safely assume that it is in a sense our own choice. God, if indeed He exists, does not put us into circumstances to try us, or to test our mettle – *we decide them for ourselves*.

It doesn't seem to me that God – the supreme spirit, or whatever you like to call him, her or it – intervenes much in human affairs. I'm not sure now whether I believe in some kind of supreme spirit – I still haven't any convincing evidence for such a personage – but if there is such a force, I believe that it does not operate on the material sphere.

My recent belief in reincarnation has profoundly changed many of my previous ideas. It has also given me a far more charitable, less envious outlook on the world. I am no longer jealous of people who have been born into better circumstances than myself, who are cleverer, better-looking or generally more privileged. Like most people, I am aware that there are people who have been born into vastly better circumstances than myself, and also that many thousands exist in far worse conditions. I now believe that all of us have earned our present circumstances and successes or failures, illness or health.

This doesn't necessarily mean that we always like our circumstances, but at least we can understand that we have no need to blame our parents or other people for what we appear to have missed in life. It's not their fault. It's not our fault, either. It's not anybody's fault – it's the way it is.

But I also believe that in each incarnation we can make something of our lives. We do not have to stay in the circumstances in which we find ourselves. We have free will and we have intelligence, and we can change our lives for the better – if we are able to learn important lessons. It does seem as though we are condemned to repeat things until we learn the lessons.

A belief in reincarnation has also given me a very different outlook on the family. When one accepts rebirth, such things as genealogy and family trees become nonsense. All that parents do is to enable a new soul to come into another incarnation by providing a body. My children are not 'mine' – they are age-old souls for whom I have temporary responsibility. It is possible that in another life they were my parents, my neighbours, my cousins, uncles or aunts. It doesn't matter, and we can never know for sure. But now I realize that I am not responsible for their characters, or for what they do in life. They are responsible for themselves, and there is very little that I can do to help them along the way. I can clothe and feed them, try to provide them with a happy home environment and a good education, but I can never do anything to guarantee that they will be happy or successful.

If children don't turn out as expected, parents should never ask themselves where they have gone wrong, or feel blame or guilt. The parents do what they can – if they are inadequate, they can't really help it. A belief in reincarnation means that negative emotions such as blame or guilt fly out of the window.

The idea of *karma* – this Eastern concept for which we have no corresponding Western word – enables us to interpret human actions in a completely different way, and to take a much wider and longer perspective. Some people have objected that if we believe in reincarnation and *karma* we accept everything as it is and never make any effort.

In fact, the opposite should happen. Once we accept the reality of reincarnation, we can then make more effort – to try to live our lives in as good a way as possible, and to avoid causing sorrow to others and creating negative *karma* which will inevitably rebound on ourselves in some adverse way.

Those who believe in reincarnation know that they cannot wound or kill somebody without the consequences of that action coming back to them eventually. The related doctrines of *karma* and rebirth also help to explain otherwise unexplainable illnesses and misfortunes. Many hypnotherapists who have regressed people say that a person who is blind in this life will often reveal a past life where he blinded somebody. In other words, there is a reason for everything. It's not God punishing us, but we who have brought our present circumstances about by our own actions. This idea, to me, makes complete sense.

My belief in reincarnation has not come about through any personal revelations or mystic happenings of any kind. I have never had any spiritual experiences or forceful moments of *déjà vu*. I have never seen a ghost or an apparition, never gone into a trance, never had any personal intimation of a past life. So for me, coming to this belief has been a purely intellectual exercise. Like most people with reasonably enquiring minds, I like to have a satisfying explanation of why we are here, what we are doing and where we are going – what the point of it all is.

I don't pretend to know the intricacies of the reincarnation process. Although it seems reasonable to suppose that we incarnate into fertilized human embryos, I have no idea when and how this happens. Some people believe that the soul enters at the time of conception, others that it happens some time during the pregnancy, and yet others a minute or two after the baby is born. We don't see it happening because it is all non-material.

Nor have I any idea how long after physical death we reincarnate. Again, there are widely differing teachings on this aspect. Some belief systems say that we incarnate again instantly, others that a period of a hundred years or so elapses. I think it is likely that we incarnate quickly, and this is borne out by Professor Ian Stevenson's investigations – otherwise the doctrine of *karma* and the whole point of reincarnation would be lost. If we have to live out the consequences, good or bad, of a previous life, surely we would do so quickly; after a hundred years or more, circumstances would have changed so much that we might no longer be able to do it.

I don't know, either, what happens to souls between one incarnation and the other. I don't know where they go, or just how it is decided what kind of body they will inhabit next. There are, again, widely differing beliefs on this, and of course we can never know for sure what happens.

So do all souls reincarnate? And where do new ones keep coming from, as the population keeps increasing? Dr Denys Kelsey believes that there is an infinite number of souls, so that there are always more than there are bodies to inhabit. The Brahma Kumaris Spiritual University – whose teachings on reincarnation make more sense than any others I have come across – say that although new souls are coming down all the time, there is a fixed number. When all the souls are 'used up', they say, there will be a nuclear holocaust. This will ensure that most, although not all, of humanity is wiped out, and that most souls will go back to the spirit world. Then we will enter into a new golden age, the time remembered in the ancient scriptures, and the whole process will start again. Dinosaurs and such animals, they say, are genetic mutations brought about by radiation.

The Brahma Kumaris also say that humans have always been humans, and were never plants, fishes or monkeys. For them, as for many Eastern religions, time is circular, not linear. The idea of Darwinian-type evolution is hard to square with the doctrines of reincarnation and *karma*, as it theorizes that humans have once been lowly organisms and are constantly evolving. But if we can accept the idea that time might be circular, we can see how the human soul is eternal – it did not come into existence at one particular point, but has always existed. It is the same with God, for those who believe that there must be some supreme intelligence at the head of everything – God has always existed and always will.

I'm not sure how far I can go along with this, but the idea that there are 'new' and 'old' souls both explains the constant rise in population, and the fact that some people do seem 'newer' than others. As a general rule, those people who seem happy and uncomplicated, who are good-looking and successful without any apparent effort, are usually thought to be 'new' souls. 'Old' souls are those who tend to be brooding and melancholy and to have complicated personalities that are difficult to relate to. Most parents and teachers have noticed that some children seem curiously old and precocious: these might be 'old' souls who have incarnated many times.

Another aspect which went some way to converting me to reincarnation was that, although the body grows old and changes visibly, we never seem to feel any different 'inside'. As novelist Shirley Conran once said, we always feel seventeen in our heads. Whenever octogenarians are asked whether they feel old they invariably reply no – that although they can see that their bodies have become frail and elderly, inside they feel the same as ever.

Some religions teach that we incarnate in order to perfect ourselves so that we can eventually go to Heaven for ever, and no longer need to experience life on earth. We go to Heaven for ever, they say, when we have learned all the lessons we need to learn. To me, this doctrine does not make much sense. For one thing, it is readily observable that human beings generally are not getting any better: there is little improvement, and many people believe quite the reverse – that everything is constantly deteriorating. Certainly, people are still fighting and killing each other and we have not learned to live in global harmony. I think it is probable that some people are learning their lessons, while others are not; not all of us are improving, although some of us might be.

To me now, the doctrine of reincarnation gives by far the better explanation of how the world works than any other I have come across. I can't be absolutely certain, of course, but now I am *reasonably* certain that it happens.

I cannot of course prove that either Lee Ward or Soozi Holbeche really saw or made me see into my past lives when I went to see them. I have no choice but to take it all on trust, although I now believe that it is quite possible that the 'Akashic records' do exist in some cosmic, non-material plane. I also believe it is possible that ghosts and apparitions may be earthbound spirits, although I am reserving judgment on this one. Until I have seen a ghost or witnessed an apparition, or the evidence for their existence becomes stronger, I can't whole-heartedly go along with the 'earthbound spirit' theory. We still don't understand all the whys and wherefores, but I am now convinced there is too much evidence of one kind and another to support reincarnation for us in the West to rule it out any longer.

# BIBLIOGRAPHY

**Bek, Lilla and Pullar, Philippa**
*The Seven Levels of Healing*
Rider, 1986


**Cott, Jonathan**
*The Search for Omm Sety: Reincarnation and Eternal Love*
Rider, 1988


**Dinnage, Rosemary**
*Annie Besant*
Penguin, 1986


**Ellison, Arthur**
*The Reality of the Paranormal*
Harrap, 1988

**Evans, Hilary**
*Visions, Apparitions, Alien Visitors*
Aquarian, 1984

**Gallup, George**
*Adventures in Immortality*
Corgi, 1984

**Gauld, Alan**
*Mediumship and Survival*
Heinemann, for the Society for Psychical Research, 1983

**Gordon, Henry**
*Channeling into the New Age: The Teachings of Shirley Maclaine and other such gurus*
Prometheus Books, 1988

**Grant, Joan**
*Winged Pharaoh*
Sphere, 1973

*Life as Carola*
Sphere, 1973

*So Moses Was Born*
Avon, New York, 1969

*Eyes of Horus*
Corgi, 1975

*Lord of the Horizon*
Avon, New York, 1969

*Far Memory*
Corgi, 1975

**Grant, Joan, and Kelsey, Denys**
*Many Lifetimes*
Doubleday, New York, 1967

**Grey, Margot**
*Return from Death*
Arkana, 1985

**Guirdham, Arthur**
*The Cathars and Reincarnation. The Record of*
*a Past Life in Thirteenth-Century France.*
Turnstone Press, 1970


**Haraldsson, Erlendur, PhD**
*Miracles are my Visiting Cards – an investigative report on the*
*psychic phenomena associated with Sai Baba*
Rider, 1986


**Hartley, Christine**
*The Case for Reincarnation*
Robert Hale, 1986


**Harvey, David, ed**
*Thorson's Complete Guide to Alternative Living*
Thorsons, 1985


**Hawken, Paul**
*The Magic of Findhorn*
Fontana, 1976


**Head, Joseph and Cranston, S.L.**
*Reincarnation: The Phoenix Fire Mystery*
Julian Press/Crown Publishers Inc. New York, 1977


**Hubbard, Ron**
*Have You Lived Before this Life?*
Scientology Publications Organisation, 1950


**Klimo, Jon**
*Channeling: Investigations on Receiving Information*
*from Paranormal Sources*
Aquarian, 1988

**Mackenzie, Andrew**
*Hauntings and Apparitions*
Heinemann, for the Society for Psychical Research, 1982

**Mackenzie, Vicki**
*Reincarnation: The Boy Lama*
Bloomsbury, 1988

**Maclaine, Shirley**
*Out on a Limb*
Elm Tree Books, 1983

**Mills, Hayley, and Maclaine, Marcus**
*My God*
Pelham Books, 1988

**Muktananda, Swami**
*Does Death Really Exist?*
Siddha Yoga Dham America Foundation, 1981

**Pullar, Philippa**
*Spiritual and Lay Healing*
Penguin, 1988

**Rampa, Lobsang**
*The Third Eye*
Secker and Warburg, 1957

*Chapters of Life*
Corgi, 1967

**Rogo, D. Scott**
*The Infinite Boundary*
Aquarian, 1988

*The Return from Silence*
Thorsons, 1989

**Stevenson, Ian**
*Twenty Cases Suggestive of Reincarnation*
University of Virginia Press, 1974

*Children Who Remember Previous Lives*
University of Virginia Press, 1987


**Weiss, Brian**
*Many Lives, Many Masters*
Simon and Schuster, 1989

# INDEX